What's Wrong with Outreach

Reexamining Evangelism, Discipleship, and the Purpose of Christian Life

Keith Edwin Schooley

Print Edition:

ISBN-13: 978-1481063463
ISBN-10: 1481063464

for my love Cecile
who's always believed in me
no matter the cost

Dear Georgia,

Thank you so much for your support and encouragement as I wrote this. God bless you now and always.

Keith

Acknowledgments:

I am deeply grateful to my wife Cecile and to my good friends Bob Mitton, Chris Lambert, and John Pop for their support, encouragement, and invaluably helpful suggestions during the process of writing and editing this book for publication. Needless to say, their support and encouragement does not imply agreement with everything written here.

Contents

Introduction

"I had the strangest dream last night. I was standing in front of a door with a sign on it. I pushed and pushed on that door. I pushed and pushed on it, but no matter how hard I pushed, I couldn't get it open."
"What did the sign say?"
"It said Pull."

The evangelical church has been pushing on the door of outreach for decades. It has organized evangelistic crusades, taught evangelism strategies, run homeless shelters, food pantries, and soup kitchens, put on concerts, sporting events, and movies to draw in unchurched people, done special service projects and outreach events, handed out bottles of water at public gatherings and conducted reverse confessionals.

All of this has been done with minimal success.

Books are written and seminars are conducted to explain what's wrong and to promote some new strategy. There are always better ways to connect with younger generations. There are new angles on reproducing the types of ministry we find in the gospels and in Acts. There are new strategies: how to witness to your friends, how to form intentional friendships to reach people for Christ, how to spot people who would be open, how to reach out to the poor, how to live among people so that your life is a witness, how to draw people into the church, how to get the church to live out Christ in the community, how to minister to people's felt needs.

But no matter how many seminars are offered and books are written, the impact is spotty. A church will have success with one method or another, and that will become the new trend for a few years, until it is found by painful experience that the success doesn't seem very reproducible and people flock to another method.

Both pastors and laypeople get burned out by the process. Always trying another strategy, always seeking the same elusive goal, gets old after a while. Failure is tiring. But because we're committed to the idea of outreach and evangelism, because we believe that that's what the church was instituted for, we keep pushing on that door. What else is there to do?

It's possible that God has given us a sign: the Bible. The problem is that we're already trying to implement what we believe the Bible is saying to us; we feel that the imperative to outreach is the Bible's message, and so we keep pushing on the door. But maybe, just maybe, we need to reread the sign.

It might be telling us that the whole approach is wrong, that not only our means and methodology and strategies are wrong, but that the actual aims are wrong, that we have the wrong focus, that we've substituted a part of the picture for the whole thing, and that if we got the rest of the picture into focus, we would find that the outreach portion takes much better care of itself.

It might be telling us to stop pushing, and instead, pull.

That is what this book is about. It's a reexamination of what the Bible actually has to say about outreach and evangelism, in the larger context of what the Christian life is supposed to be about and how the body of Christ is supposed to function together. What does the Great Commission really entail? How did the church go about its remarkable expansion in the book of Acts? What do the epistles tell us about the duties of ordinary believers regarding outreach? What really is our ultimate goal as believers? What part do spiritual gifts play? What is the relationship between evangelism and discipleship? Why did the early church, and churches under persecution, grow so much more rapidly than churches that are more established and free to reach out? How can we rediscover what part outreach has to play in the larger scheme of what the overall Christian life is supposed to be?

This isn't a simple how-to book. We can't reorient our direction with a bulleted list of action items. We don't need mere superficial change; we need to alter our idea of what the Christian life is all about. So be prepared for concentrated reading, soul searching, and challenges to some basic assumptions we've all grown up with. My plea is for a hearing, an honest appraisal of whether how we go about church and outreach are, in fact, biblical. Or is there a better way?

TV News

We can learn a lot about the problems of the contemporary church by examining a seemingly unlikely source: television news.

Broadcast television news viewership has been declining for many years. There are several reasons: competition from 24-hour cable news outlets, the rise of news accessibility on the internet, and increasingly popular opinion-based news coverage appearing on all types of media. Present-day viewership is now less than half of what it was in 1980.

During the same time period, increasing pressure has been brought to bear on television news outlets to become financially self-sustaining. Once considered a public service by broadcasters, television news divisions have become subject to the same pressures as their entertainment divisions: generate advertising revenue by increasing ratings and market share. This has led to a trend toward so-called "soft news"—lifestyle, celebrity, and human-interest stories that function more as entertainment than serious information. Networks found that soft news stories would increase market share, especially when promoted heavily with teasers, so they pushed their news departments to air growing amounts of soft news, often over the objections of veteran journalists.

While soft news might have made temporary market share gains for individual news programs, the overall trend for news viewership has continued to decline. It's possible that the decline was inevitable, given competition from various technologies, and may not have been halted no matter what content individual news providers offered. Nonetheless, trying to increase news viewership by including an enlarging proportion of soft news involves a fundamental contradiction. While those who don't usually watch the news might be drawn in by recipes that encourage weight loss or the latest developments in a celebrity's love life, serious news viewers are likely to consider the same stories a waste of time. Those serious news viewers are then likely to search for alternative ways of getting news and information. Meanwhile, casual news viewers, lured into watching a particular show based on a particular story, have no enduring interest in watching the news on an ongoing basis. There have to be continual soft-news lures to keep those viewers engaged, while those who would have been likely to be loyal have been alienated.

Soft news stories do not simply use up time that hard-news viewers find pointless. They also limit the time, and therefore the depth, of the hard news that gets covered. Sometimes news organizations acknowledge that their reporting of serious topics is increasingly superficial and driven by sound bites. They complain that it is impossible to cover news subjects in depth given the limits of a half-hour program. But if that's true, it makes even less sense of the time that is devoted to soft news. If it is difficult to squeeze all the news of a day into 22 minutes of non-commercial time in a broadcast, why spend half of that time on subjects that are not truly timely and significant?

The strategy that seemed to create a short-term increase in news viewership is likely to have contributed to its long-term decline. This conflict between short-term strategies and long-term results is evident in many different endeavors. Politicians find that running negative ads is effective in defeating an opponent in a particular election, but the result of all candidates running negative ads is an increasing level of popular disgust with politicians in general. Investors and corporate executives make decisions based on short-term profit potential without regard to long-term effects. When this occurs throughout an industry, consequences such as the early 2000s housing bubble occur. Mortgages were then being written with little thought regarding ability to repay, since they were being bundled and sold off for short-term profit. Repayment was going to be someone else's problem, until the bubble burst in 2008, and it all became everyone's problem.

So what does all this have to do with the church?

The role of the local church has also been in decline in recent decades. This has led to an increasing trend of strategies designed to reach out and draw in more people, from contemporary worship styles to seeker-sensitive service formats to emergent and missional church models. All of these developments have merits which could be debated individually; the point here is that all of them start from the premise that the main point of the church is outreach. This starting point is all-but-inevitable given the evangelical emphasis on the Great Commission as the overriding missions statement of the church. Our mission is to "make disciples," which necessarily entails an outward focus. It mandates that we do whatever is likely to draw people in and bring them to saving faith. This seems to make sense, but the overall effect appears to be continued decline. Is it possible that the church has fallen into a similar trap as broadcast news?

There are obvious differences, of course. Church services and ministries should not be designed merely to retain the loyalty of those who already attend. Many churches function in exactly that way, and it results in dwindling congregations that cater to the tastes of their long-term members while children and grandchildren flee. But when the church sees outreach as its primary mission, it misses the point of what outreach is for. People temporarily attracted because of a special event, a topical series focused on practical felt needs, or a service project for the community, are unlikely to continue to attend, let alone get involved in the life of the church, once the initial hook has run its course and the church has moved on to other things.

The goal of outreach is usually conceived of as bringing those who were previously outsiders to a commitment to Jesus for salvation. This is a noble goal, as far as it goes, but once people have had a salvation experience, they are naturally going to ask the question, Now what? And this is where many churches have little serious guidance for new believers. They will be advised to read the Bible and pray daily, and perhaps to fast or participate in other spiritual disciplines. There will be pressure to conform to the church's social standards regarding dress, language, church participation, and tobacco and alcohol use. New believers will be instructed on particular areas of morality (primarily sexual in nature) that are considered non-negotiable. And then, there's not much else.

Except, of course, the mandate to go out and reach more of the lost. It will often be stated baldly that the only reason a person continues to live on planet Earth after having received salvation is to bring other people to heaven. So when the church views its mission solely in terms of fulfilling the Great Commission, and the Great Commission in terms of bringing "the lost" to a point of salvation, and salvation as something whose main purpose (in this life, anyway) is to turn around and reach more people, then the entire process ends up looking increasingly like a multi-level marketing scheme. And to a generation that has been marketed to death and has become very leery of marketing schemes, all this is a turn-off. The process that focuses on reaching people ends up having the effect of pushing them away.

This is how the church's outreach efforts, whatever form they take, end up becoming as counterproductive as TV soft news. The problem is always thought to be one of methodology, and books get churned out regularly as pastors of churches that have some success with some method advise others on how it has been achieved. If only we find the right method, if only we make the Christian faith more relevant to the world around us, if only we capture how to do what Jesus did and contextualize it properly for our culture, then we'll manage to reach the lost in an effective way.

But the problem is not one of methodology; it's one of goals. The means are not the issue; the end is. TV news lost its way because it saw its mission as garnering more viewers, instead of delivering the news—the real news—to whomever would watch. Similarly, the church has lost its way because it sees its mission as reaching more people, instead of delivering the news—the Good News—to whomever will listen. Of course, TV news can present the news in a more or less engaging way, and there's nothing wrong with trying to make the presentation more engaging. Similarly, the church can present the gospel in a more or less engaging way, and there's nothing wrong with trying to make that presentation more engaging. But the heart of the matter is the gospel, not how many people are being reached.

This issue becomes obvious when we consider churches that appear to be reaching large numbers of people with a defective or absent gospel message. Most of us will not recognize ourselves to be in the same category, particularly if our theology is orthodox and we present the message of the Cross as substitutionary atonement. But if the ends are focused on bringing people in, without much thought to what to do with them once they are in, or why (other than being saved from hell) someone should want to be in at all, then there's really very little difference. The message offered by most of our churches may not be a defective gospel, but it is certainly a shallow gospel, and the world is hungry for depth. What happens when a person who is searching for meaning comes to a church, only to find that "meaning" consists of repeat this prayer, help with this project, follow this set of social conventions? He or she is likely to leave, and as Jesus once said, "The last state is worse than the first." If approached again, the person is likely to say, "Oh, I tried that already. Didn't work for me." They've been inoculated to the gospel—and there are millions of people like that. Without meaning to, the church's efforts at outreach are ghettoizing it as a subculture that appears irrelevant to the rest of the world.

None of this should be interpreted as meaning that outreach is unimportant, that the Great Commission is irrelevant, or that salvation for the lost is an unworthy goal. The greatest TV news program ever will be irrelevant if no one watches it. The point being made here is that outreach must be focused on a goal beyond itself, that the Great Commission involves much more than reaching "the lost," and that salvation is a process that goes far beyond the point we might call conversion. If we get straight on the ends, the way to go about the means will be much more clear. If we figure out the actual role of the church and where the Great Commission fits into it, we'll be able to live out that role, and accomplish the Great Commission, much better. If we determine where we're going with people once they've made a commitment to Jesus, we'll be much better able to steer them toward him from the beginning.

The answers to all of this lie in scripture. We generally think that our present, defective way of going about evangelism is scripturally based; but in fact it is the result of taking a few passages out of context and making them the center of how we go about doing church. If we get scripture back in balance and follow that, our evangelistic efforts will come back in line.

I'm not suggesting that we can do an end run around the problem, that deconstructing outreach as we know it today will result in the key to unlock outreach and draw in hordes of people. Stopping the numbers game as a goal is not a clever way of winning the numbers game. I do think that looking at outreach in a more biblical way will make doing it more fruitful—that those who were reached would be more deeply and permanently transformed, as I think was Jesus' goal—but it won't necessarily draw in large numbers of people. What Jesus said about the narrow and wide roads may hold true no matter what we do. But our first step must be to make Jesus' goals our goals. And then the rest that follows will be exactly what he planned.

The Great Commission

The Great Commission is one of the most frequently referred-to passages in the Bible. I'm also convinced that it is one of the most misunderstood and misapplied. Let's look at the text:

> Then the eleven disciples went to Galilee, to the mountain where Jesus had told them to go. When they saw him, they worshiped him; but some doubted. Then Jesus came to them and said, "All authority in heaven and on earth has been given to me. Therefore go and make disciples of all nations, baptizing them in the name of the Father and of the Son and of the Holy Spirit, and teaching them to obey everything I have commanded you. And surely I am with you always, to the very end of the age."
>
> Matthew 28:16-20

The common evangelical interpretation of the Commission involves several features. First, the Commission is understood to be the driving missions statement of the church—its placement at the end of Matthew's gospel, spoken by the post-resurrection Jesus, makes it clear that this is Jesus' mandate to all who follow him. Second, evangelicals apply the Commission to all believers individually: it is each disciple's responsibility to live out this mandate in his or her life. Third, the Commission is directed specifically toward reaching the lost—that is, bringing people to saving faith in Jesus. It is generally understood in terms of rescuing people from an eternity in hell. Finally, the Commission is primarily accomplished by personal witnessing—sharing one's faith with others—in combination with supporting preaching and missionary ministries (or directly engaging in such ministries), sometimes also in combination with such "pre-evangelism" activities as service projects that are intended to gain a receptive hearing for the gospel.

All of these features contain elements of truth, and challenging them runs the risk of being misunderstood as being unconcerned about those who are lost. Nonetheless, this understanding of the Commission actually hinders the work of evangelism in the long run, and presents a reductive and superficial view of the Christian life and of the role of the Church in the world.

First of all, it's worth at least questioning whether the importance of the Commission has been overstated by the evangelical church. This suggestion will be considered heresy to some, but it's dangerous to regard any passage as the lens through which the rest of scripture, and the rest of Christian life, is viewed. It's rare for any verse to give us an explicit window on our interpretation of the Bible as a whole. The closest one gets to that is Jesus' statement about the commands to love God and love one's neighbor, "All the Law and the Prophets hang on these two commandments" (Matt. 22:40), or Paul's statement to Timothy regarding inspiration: "All Scripture is God-breathed and is useful for teaching, rebuking, correcting and training in righteousness" (2 Tim. 3:16). There's nothing like that in the context of the Commission. Arguments have been made for the central importance of other passages as well, such as John 3:16, Romans 1:16-17 or Acts 1:8 (which is often paired with the Commission and interpreted in a similar light), but once again, overemphasis on these verses has a tendency to distort our understanding of the rest of scripture, and leads to misapplication of the passages themselves.

All this is not to deny that the Great Commission is placed in such a way as to be the capstone of Matthew's gospel. Clearly, Jesus meant it as an imperative to the eleven, and by extension, to the Church that was to follow. Evidently, Matthew meant, by including it, to point to the spread of the gospel that had already taken place by the time that he penned it, and to encourage its further spread. Nonetheless, Matthew is only one of four gospels, and this particular episode is not recorded in the other three, unlike other events such as the feeding of the five thousand or Peter's confession of faith, which are emphasized by their inclusion in all four gospels. The final climactic event included in every gospel is, of course, the Resurrection. After that point, each gospel writer concludes the narrative in a way that emphasizes his own highlighted themes. It's bad interpretation to impose Matthew's closing focus on each of the other gospels, much less on the Christian life as a whole.

This misplaced emphasis becomes more clear when we read Acts and the epistles to see how the actual missionary impulse was fulfilled in the early church. In Acts, we see an amazing expansion of the church in the thirty years or so after Jesus' resurrection. Nonetheless, as we will see, Acts doesn't apply the Great Commission by highlighting personal evangelism in the way evangelicals usually do. It does draw attention to two things: remarkable growth, especially in the early chapters, largely based on outsiders' perception of the believers' character; and a divinely-empowered evangelistic ministry, primarily focused on Peter, Philip, and Paul—that is to say, focused on a small group of specific people who are gifted and charged with the task of spreading the gospel.

In the epistles, we see issues that occurred in the early church and needed to be addressed. The epistles are all occasional documents, most of them dealing with particular struggles and problems that were faced by the early church. They deal with such varied topics as legalism (Galatians), insufficient focus on Jesus (Colossians), division, rivalry, class distinction, misuse of spiritual gifts, using prostitutes, and incest (1 Corinthians). With all of these problems afflicting the early church, one would think that a breakdown of personal evangelism would be among the hot topics addressed, yet there is not a single word of encouragement, instruction, or admonishment regarding the responsibility of individual believers to evangelize. The closest one gets to that is Paul's appeal for support of his own missionary activity in Romans 10—but that is an appeal for believers to support him, not for them to carry out the missionary work themselves. What one repeatedly sees is an appeal to live exemplary lives so that the gospel will gain a favorable hearing among unbelievers in the larger populace. Some people explain the lack of encouragement to witness by asserting that it was unnecessary, given such a great enthusiasm for Jesus among the early Christian community. Yet it seems impossible to imagine that over the course of several decades, during which all of the above corruptions of the gospel were taking place, neglect of evangelism somehow never occurred or needed to be addressed.

The record of Acts and the epistles leads to an inescapable conclusion, if we are willing to look at it: the Commission simply does not apply to each particular believer, at least not in the way evangelicals typically take it. It turns out that we can't simply lift the Commission out of its historical context and apply it to everyone individually. What we need to do when applying the passage is to look at the people Jesus was actually speaking to, and see whom they might represent.

Matthew 28:16 makes clear that Jesus addressed the Commission to "the eleven disciples," i.e., the twelve minus Judas Iscariot. The people they could reasonably be supposed to represent are:

1. Only themselves. This would make the Commission into a simple historical narrative: Jesus is merely telling those who were closest to him in his earthly life what their mission is, now that he is about to be gone. In this view, it would have no further application in the present day.

2. Church leaders. In this view, the apostles represent later elders and overseers—the leadership
   of the church. The charge to make disciples
   therefore would be the responsibility of the ordained clergy. This might fit nicely with a high-
   church polity that makes a significant distinction between clergy and laity.

3. All believers individually. The eleven here simply stand in for all believers in generations to
   come. This is the view of the evangelical church
   as the Commission is usually taught. In this
   view, it is the responsibility of each one of us
   personally to win as many people as possible to
   salvation.

4. The whole church corporately. The eleven here
   stand for the church as a whole, but not every
   aspect of the Commission applies equally to
   each individual person. The church as a whole
   is charged with the commission, and each individual plays his own part in carrying it out.

The first option, taking the Commission as a historical
narrative without present-day application, has rarely if ever
been advocated. Aside from the fact that biblical history is
almost always recognized as having an importance beyond
its immediate context, the placement of the Commission
at the end of Matthew's Gospel demands response from
the reader. Nothing in the passage suggests that Jesus'
words should apply only to his immediate listeners. There
is nothing specifically cultural or personal about the
Commission (in contrast with such statements as "Greet

one another with a holy kiss" or "Bring me the cloak I left at Troas"). And the very nature of the Gospels as they are written seems to demand a larger application to Jesus' words, particularly to his instructions to the disciples. What would be the point of Matthew relating the five great discourses in his Gospel if they did not relate at least to his own immediate audience, already separated from the events described by several decades? So the Commission applies to a group larger than the eleven to whom it was immediately addressed.

It's possible that some may functionally choose the second option, that the eleven represent church leadership, especially in denominations that maintain a strong distinction between clergy and laity, but this view is seldom advocated explicitly. Passages such as 1 Timothy 3 or Titus 1 that discuss the qualifications and responsibilities of church leadership do not focus on evangelism. Few would dispute that evangelism can and should be undertaken by a wider circle of people than the ordained clergy—indeed, the people most gifted for evangelism might not even include some people who are actually called to minister in other capacities full-time.

Option three is the commonly held assumption in evangelical churches, and the one which I've already attempted to refute: namely, that evangelism is everyone's responsibility individually. Simply put, there is actually very little about overt evangelism in the New Testament, compared with the central importance that the evangelical church has placed on it. Not in the Gospels, apart from the Commission and from the Kingdom proclamation undertaken by Jesus personally and by the twelve and the seventy—that is, by specific people selected by Jesus from among the multitudes that were following him. Not in Acts, which focuses on the character of the new believers and on the evangelistic efforts of a specific small group of people divinely called and appointed for the task. Not in the epistles, which deal with all sorts of different problematic issues going on in the church, but never once charge all believers individually with the task of evangelism.

Because of this dearth of actual material in the New Testament, contemporary exhortations toward evangelism tend to focus on a few passages, like the Commission, and lean heavily on rhetoric describing masses of lost people hurtling toward an eternity in hell. Don't we care about them? Don't we have the heart of Jesus toward them? Can you imagine your friends/coworkers/neighbors/family members, in line for the White Throne Judgment, looking at you with tears in their eyes, asking you, "Why didn't you tell me?" Surely, even if evangelism is not dealt with in so many words, isn't it still implied by the overall narrative and the clear missionary impulse that underlies the entire New Testament?

If there were no other options, then I would say Yes. It is, simply put, the heart of Jesus to care about the lost. But the fourth option listed above recognizes the nature of the Body as a group of differently-gifted individuals who don't each do the same thing but all work together toward a common goal. It also takes seriously what the Commission states about making disciples—not merely making converts. Finally, it makes sense of the wording of the

Commission itself, which (in combination with other passages) actually precludes the idea that the Commission is directed toward every believer individually.

As has often been noted, the active verb controlling the sentence structure of the Commission is the one translated "make disciples." "Go" is a participle that is probably coordinate with it—that is, it takes on the force of a command, along with "make disciples." It has been suggested that "go" should be made subordinate to "make disciples," leading to a translation like "as you go, disciple people" (ISV); but it appears that whether Jesus is telling his disciples to go or merely assuming that they will go, some sort of movement toward those who are not yet disciples is implied. Historically, the church largely remained in Jerusalem until persecution broke out against it (Acts 8:1). Evidently, the providence of God and the world's hostility toward the Gospel would conspire together to cause the church to "go" in any event.

But the focus of the Commission is to "make disciples." Those who emphasize individual responsibility in fulfilling the Commission invariably focus that phrase on evangelism of the lost and bringing people to a point of conversion. However, both the implications of making disciples (not merely converts) and the way in which Jesus fleshes out the concept in the Commission itself preclude such a narrow application. Jesus divides making disciples into two main subordinate actions: "baptizing" and "teaching." Baptism was the mode of entry into the community of believers and would thus be located more or less as the end result of the efforts that we now call "evangelism." Presumably, Jesus is putting all these efforts—pre-evangelism, witnessing, preaching, invitation, and guidance into baptism itself—under the heading of "baptism," since he can hardly be imagined to advocate baptizing unwilling people who have no idea what baptism signifies. (Even if the baptism of infants is to be allowed for, at least the evangelism of the parents must have already taken place.) Jesus states that baptism is to be done "in the name of the Father, and of the Son, and of the Holy Spirit," probably not for the purpose of establishing a baptismal formula, but to make clear that those being baptized are submitting themselves to God in all his fullness and various persons.

Teaching is the second aspect of making disciples that Jesus denotes. Its placement after "baptizing" makes it reasonably clear that already-baptized believers are to be the ones who are to be taught. Jesus states that the object of the teaching is that the disciples "obey everything I have commanded you." Some have inferred that all the teaching envisioned is to be practical, in the sense that it is basically a matter of commands to be obeyed, not doctrine to be learned. "Teaching doctrine," in these circles, is frowned upon.[1] But if we examine how the church actually carried out Jesus' mission as it appears in Acts and the epistles, it seems that just as baptism encompassed more than simply the act of baptism itself, so "teaching them to obey" involves much more than simply commands and

---

[1] In fact, "teaching doctrine" is simply redundant: "doctrine" is merely another, more old-fashioned word for "teaching." Both are used to translate the Greek word *didaskalia,* and there is no distinction in the original text.

outward compliance. The Apostle Paul, in particular, both in Acts (for example, in his address to the Ephesian elders in chapter 20) and in his epistles, not only gives commands to be carried out, but also teaches those to whom he is speaking or writing the theological "whys"—the concrete information necessary for establishing a theological basis and worldview in which the commands find their place and rationale. His letters often have a primarily doctrinal section (e.g., Romans 1-11 or Ephesians 1-3) expounding upon an aspect of the gospel needed to be understood by that church, followed by a primarily practical section (e.g., Romans 12-15 or Ephesians 4-6) describing how the truths in the doctrinal section may be practically lived out.

So in the Great Commission, Jesus divides the command to "make disciples" into "baptizing" and "teaching," two headings that evidently involve a great deal more than those terms may seem to imply on the surface. The two aspects of what Jesus commanded might in a modern context be called "evangelism" and "discipleship," although even those two terms as they are practiced today hardly do justice to the breadth of the mission Jesus was entrusting to his church. It encompasses everything from laying the groundwork in order to obtain a hearing for the gospel ("pre-evangelism") to sophisticated theological instruction and practical mentoring in living out the implications of that same gospel.

The more one recognizes the breadth of the charge that Jesus gave to his disciples, the less one can imagine that any single person is supposed to carry out all of it. It is, in fact, precluded by the text itself, viewed in light of other passages. Although Jesus states that a part of making disciples is baptizing, no less a missionary than Paul himself was able to say to one of the congregations he had founded,

> I thank God that I did not baptize any of you except Crispus and Gaius, so no one can say that you were baptized in my name. (Yes, I also baptized the household of Stephanas; beyond that, I don't remember if I baptized anyone else.) For Christ did not send me to baptize, but to preach the gospel....

1 Corinthians 1:14-17

So even though the process of evangelism should culminate in baptism, Paul himself did not physically baptize very many people. Neither did Jesus, according to John 4:2.

Similarly, making disciples also involves teaching, yet James writes, "Not many of you should become teachers, my fellow believers, because you know that we who teach will be judged more strictly" (James 3:1). So an aspect of the Great Commission, as Jesus describes it, is being recommended against by one of the most important leaders of the early church, presumably someone who is actively engaged in fulfilling the Commission himself.

So if Jesus' final command to his followers was to make disciples, and if making disciples involves both baptizing and teaching, and if leaders in the church are themselves not practicing both of them, or advocating that we not practice one of them, then the fact is inescapable: not every believer is to be engaged in every aspect of the Great Commission. Various people will be engaged in fulfilling various parts of it, but no one person will fulfill all of it.

However, this does not mean that the Commission does not apply to all believers. In fact, this should give excitement and hope to many people who feel unable to fulfill the Commission as it is typically understood. While not everyone will be involved in direct evangelistic outreach, everyone has a part to play in fulfilling the commission in a larger sense. Some will lay the groundwork by making connections to people who would be otherwise hostile or indifferent to the gospel. Some will share their own testimonies of what God has done in their lives. Some will overtly preach the message of salvation through Jesus. Some will actually shepherd people through the process of being baptized itself.[2] Some will nurture new believers in the basic aspects of living for Jesus. Some will mentor people into a deeper relationship with God. Some will speak or write things that help others develop their faith or live it out more completely. Some will come alongside and assist all of these endeavors in various ways, as supply lines physically assist an army and are an indispensible aspect of any military endeavor.

---

[2] It may appear from the way I describe baptism in this chapter that I hold to some form of baptismal regeneration. I do not. Baptism functioned in the first century as the physical act by which people expressed faith in and commitment to Christ; that is, it functioned largely as the altar call functions in many churches today. I consider the replacement of baptism with the altar call to be unfortunate, since it makes baptism into a later step, seemingly optional, taken by a person who has already been accepted as a fellow believer by the church, a meaning that baptism never has in scripture.

This is the point. In its largest sense, the Great Commission does involve everyone. Each member of the body of Christ has his or her own part to play. No one is left out; no one is unnecessary. But we all don't have to be the same sort of person, doing the same sort of thing, in order to accomplish the goal. In fact, the more we try to fit people into a cookie-cutter mold, the less able each person will be to fulfill the aspect that he or she was intended to fulfill. The entire job simply can't be done by all of us doing the same thing. And God never intended for us to even try to do it that way.

How Outreach Works, Biblically

There is no question that the early church, beginning with the day of Pentecost, grew in a remarkable geometric expansion. Present-day church leaders look at evidence from the book of Acts and bemoan the lack of similar growth in the contemporary church. If only (it is thought) we had the passion and fervor of the early church! If only the gifts of the Spirit were moving as they did back then! If only we could get our people to have the same commitment as the early believers! The book of Acts is scoured for clues regarding the methodology that produced such amazing growth in the early church; yet somehow, the results of these searches seem to produce very intentional evangelistic and outreach efforts, usually involving getting as people involved as possible. This is surprising, because Acts and the rest of the New Testament display very little in the way of congregations engaging in intentional outreach. Other than the efforts of specific people (primarily, the Apostle Paul) who were specifically called and gifted for missionary work, the entire process appears to have been completely organic.

Put simply, the growth happened as believers were living their lives as believers. It did not happen because of any intentional strategy of church leaders—once again, other than those who were specifically called and gifted for missions. The lesson to be learned from Acts appears to be so hard to receive because it tells us something we really don't want to be told: that adding people to our numbers is not directly under our control. The way to do it, it appears, is to quit trying.

The first passage in Acts that is often cited regarding growth in the early church appears in chapter two:

> They devoted themselves to the apostles' teaching and to fellowship, to the breaking of bread and to prayer. Everyone was filled with awe at the many wonders and signs performed by the apostles. All the believers were together and had everything in common. They sold property and possessions to give to anyone who had need. Every day they continued to meet together in the temple courts. They broke bread in their homes and ate together with glad and sincere hearts, praising God and enjoying the favor of all the people. And the Lord added to their number daily those who were being saved.
>
> Acts 2:42-47

Frequently, what is focused on in this passage are the first and last verses, ignoring anything in the middle. The disciples were "devoting themselves" to four things: 1) the apostles' teaching, 2) fellowship, 3) the breaking of bread, and 4) prayer. These things appear reasonably straightforward: sermons cover the teaching part, social gatherings or small groups cover the fellowship part, "breaking of bread" is thought of as either eating together or taking

Communion together, and prayer is covered either in formal prayer meetings, prayer in small groups, or individual prayer. The result, found in the final verse of the passage, is that "the Lord added to their number daily those who were being saved."

So based on this reading, it is thought by some that the key to church growth is to get these four things right—get a critical mass of participation, get a proper balance, get just the right elements or the right methods working, and growth will come. To its credit, this view does attempt to apply an organic approach to church growth—it focuses on the lives of the believers rather than on any outreach strategy—but it misses the fuller context of the passage. Those four elements are not everything that was going on in the heady days immediately following Pentecost.

For one thing, the wonders and signs being performed by the apostles in verse 43 were drawing people in, raising the question, of course, why such miraculous signs seem to occur less frequently in the contemporary Western church. This we will return to later. But one of the most glaring issues in the passage is seldom touched: the fact that the early believers "had everything in common" and "sold property and possessions to give to anyone who had need" (vv. 44-45; something similar is also described in 4:32-35).

Political considerations tend to skew interpretations of this passage. Some decry these actions as an example of "Christian socialism" that is said to have failed and led to repeated poverty relief efforts on behalf of the Jerusalem believers (Acts 11:29-30; 1 Cor. 16:1-3; 2 Cor. 8-9).

Others positively contrast this example of "voluntary" assistance to the poor with state-imposed assistance. Of course, the implication of the word "voluntary" is that one may opt out, or limit one's participation to circumstances in which it is convenient, which is hardly the point of the passage in Acts.

The narrative itself is not concerned with any of these political considerations. Luke here appears to be simply stating a fact regarding what the early believers did, which in turn seems to be a vivid expression of Jesus' statement that the world would know his disciples by their love for one another (John 13:35). Note that this love is not merely an emotion to be felt, but something that is actually expressed in concrete ways, and that it is expressed by the disciples toward one another, not to outsiders as an outreach effort. People doubtless saw the sacrificial love being shown among the group of disciples and were drawn at least to take the new movement seriously.

This passage in Acts never states that the Lord "adding to their number" is a direct result of everything that the disciples had just been described as doing; in fact, the growth being attributed to the Lord, rather than to the believers' efforts, seems to argue against a simple cause and effect relationship. The most that can be said with confidence is that the actions of the disciples were coordinate with the growth—they might have helped it, they certainly didn't impede it, but the Lord, not the actions themselves, actually caused it. It appears clear that these actions were not taken as a means to make growth happen, and wouldn't have been abandoned if they hadn't "worked." Living as the disciples did was an organic expression of the transformation that had occurred in their lives. It wasn't an intentional means to achieve an ulterior end.

The things Jesus commanded his disciples to do weren't means to an end at all: they were ends themselves. Frequently when churches attempt to apply the "four element solution" and it doesn't produce immediate results in terms of drawing more people in, the approach is quietly forgotten and replaced by a more "intentional" method. The reality is that each of the four elements described in Acts 2:42 is an important part of the larger transformation of making disciples, whether or not it involves getting more people in the door for services. But they certainly do not exhaust the expression of that trans-formation. If we want to apply the lessons of Acts to the contemporary world, and thereby influence those who do not know Jesus, the first step might be in recognizing how deep that transformation should go and how significantly it should change our relationships with one another.

The next passage in Acts that specifically refers to people being added to the new group of disciples is in chapter 5, just after the divine judgment of Ananias and Sapphira:

> The apostles performed many signs and won-ders among the people. And all the believers used to meet together in Solomon's Colonnade. No one else dared join them, even though they were highly regarded by the people. Nevertheless, more and more men and women believed in the Lord and

were added to their number. As a result, people brought the sick into the streets and laid them on beds and mats so that at least Peter's shadow might fall on some of them as he passed by. Crowds gathered also from the towns around Jerusalem, bringing their sick and those tormented by impure spirits, and all of them were healed.

Acts 5:12-16

Here we have the theme of miraculous healings strongly tied to the growth of the early church. This continues the pattern of miraculous signs that occurred in Jesus' ministry, and fulfill what he had told his immediate disciples, that "whoever believes in me will do the works I have been doing, and they will do even greater things than these" (John 14:12). Believers from various theological backgrounds will come to differing conclusions regarding the apparent lack of such miraculous signs today, ranging from a strongly dispensational viewpoint, holding that such "temporary sign gifts" ended with the passing of the original apostles, to a strongly charismatic viewpoint, arguing that such miraculous signs only ended because of unbelief and are now occurring once again in great numbers. It is undeniable that much of the growth of the Christian church today is occurring in the Third World, and is taking place with a strongly Pentecostal flavor and with a great many reported miracles taking place.

Most believers would take the frequency of miraculous signs as being based on components of both divine sovereignty and human response. Looking at biblical history, we see long stretches of time with few reported miraculous signs, interspersed with brief but significant bursts of miraculous activity. We also see that God responded to similar situations in very different ways. The God that rained down plagues on the Egyptians and parted the Red Sea, fed the Israelites manna in the wilderness, parted the Jordan River and tore down the walls of Jericho, nonetheless made the Israelites fight their way into the Promised Land and drive out its inhabitants themselves, and allowed them to fail to complete that mission. The period documented in the books of Kings and Chronicles had little miraculous activity apart from the flourishing of miracles in the ministries of Elijah and Elisha. God miraculously delivered Peter from prison, despite an obvious lack of confidence on the part of those praying for his release (Acts 12), but allowed Paul to remain in prison for four years in Caesarea and Rome (Acts 24:27, 28:30). Certainly God's sovereign hand is involved in this. Yet we are also told that Jesus could not heal many people in his home town because of their unbelief (Mark 6:5-6).

It may be that modern Western rationalism has deeply eroded faith in the miraculous, even among those who trust in Jesus for salvation. It may be that we are another evil and adulterous generation to whom God will not show a sign. It may be that we need to repent. Or it may be that this is simply a period and a place in which God has not chosen to do many miracles. Or it may be that we forget that the Bible covers 2000 years of history from Abraham in Canaan to John on Patmos, and the miracles that it records were written down in the first place because of how rare they were, even then. Perhaps comparatively few people in biblical times ever saw one. One thing is certain: miracles are not ours to engineer, whether we want them for the purposes of outreach or for any other reason. If miracles helped to spread the gospel in Acts, we also know that they are not the sole component in bringing people to faith: Jesus excoriated the inhabitants of the cities in which he had performed miracles because they did not repent (Matthew 11:20). We should pray that God confirms his gospel by performing miracles among us, as he did for Paul. But they are not something we can manufacture.

A third passage in Acts that directly refers to significant numbers of people coming to faith is in chapter 11, in the description of the fledgling church in Antioch:

Now those who had been scattered by the persecution that broke out when Stephen was killed traveled as far as Phoenicia, Cyprus and Antioch, spreading the word only among Jews. Some of them, however, men from Cyprus and Cyrene, went to Antioch and began to speak to Greeks also, telling them the good news about the Lord Jesus. The Lord's hand was with them, and a great number of people believed and turned to the Lord.

News of this reached the church in Jerusalem, and they sent Barnabas to Antioch. When he arrived and saw what the grace of God had done, he was glad and encouraged them all to remain true to the Lord with all their hearts. He was a good man,

full of the Holy Spirit and faith, and a great number
of people were brought to the Lord.

Acts 11:19-24

Here we do have a biblical example that represents the
model that contemporary churches seem either to assume
or to actively promote: purposeful overt evangelism on
the part of ordinary believers. The evangelization of
Greeks in Antioch was undertaken by "men of Cyprus
and Cyrene"—that is, evidently not by well-known apostles or other notable figures who would have been named.
A closer examination, however, reveals significant differences between what happened in this passage and church
evangelism efforts in our day.

First of all, it was only because of the scattering of
believers in the wake of Stephen's martyrdom that this
evangelization happened at all—that is to say, it was not
an intentional outreach effort on the part of the Jerusalem believers. It has been alleged, with pretty good
reason, that the believers staying in Jerusalem for as
long as they did was actually contrary to the plan of
God. Jesus had told them not to leave Jerusalem, but
rather to "wait for the gift my Father promised, which
you have heard me speak about. For...in a few days you
will be baptized with the Holy Spirit" (Acts 1:4-5). This
had happened not long after, on the day of Pentecost,
so the command to stay in Jerusalem had long since
been fulfilled by the time Stephen was martyred. But
whether or not the Jerusalem believers should have
begun evangelizing the surrounding world earlier than
they did, the fact is that this outreach to Antioch came

about not as an intentional mission but as the effect of persecution.

More importantly, the focus of Luke's narrative here is the contrast between most of those who were scattered, who shared the gospel only with fellow Jews, and the men of Cyprus and Cyrene, who began sharing it with Greeks. It appears that the Lord's hand was with them precisely because they had begun sharing the gospel with Gentiles, perhaps having taken Peter's acceptance of the conversion of Cornelius's household to heart. Luke explicitly notes that "the Lord's hand was with them," presumably because it was the Lord's purpose at this time for the gospel to spread outside its native Jewish milieu. The success of the believers' efforts seems then to have been based not on a model nor on a strategy, but on their willingness to participate in what the Lord had already demonstrated, through Peter and the household of Cornelius, that he wanted to do.

The fact that these believers are not named may make us assume that they were more numerous than they actually were: that is, we may read "men from Cyprus and Cyrene" to mean *all* the believers from Cyprus and Cyrene. This is not by any means necessary or even likely. If what we will find in the chapter on spiritual giftedness is at all true, then another view of this passage presents itself. Of those who were scattered in the wake of Stephen's martyrdom, some were gifted for evangelism and spread the word among fellow Jews (and probably some who were not especially gifted found themselves in the right circumstances and temporarily took on that role), and of the scattered believers who were from Cyprus and Cyrene, there were some who were gifted for evangelism and also had the insight to recognize that the gospel should be shared among the Gentiles. When they did so, the Lord blessed their efforts, because it was his purpose to begin spreading the gospel among Gentiles at that time. In other words, a mass evangelism effort was not being rewarded simply because everyone was getting involved; rather, God was using people to whom he had given evangelistic gifts in order to accomplish his purposes, and blessed their efforts precisely to the extent that they were directed toward his purposes.

This perspective is strengthened by the fact that much of the rest of the book of Acts is focused on the missionary efforts of a few people, clearly gifted for evangelism, and that all of the intentional outreach occurred through those few people, not through the mass efforts of believers in general.

Going back to the beginning of Acts, the first of these gifted individuals is, of course, Peter. Although Acts has been traditionally known as "The Acts of the Apostles," it actually only describes events involving three of the original twelve: Peter, James, and John—and the only action involving James is his martyrdom. Peter certainly dominates the first several chapters of Acts. It is he who preaches the Pentecost sermon, he who is used to heal the lame beggar and preaches to the crowd that gathered as a result, he who (along with John) stands up to the Sanhedrin, he who confronts Ananias and Sapphira about their deception, and he who received the vision and shared the gospel with Cornelius's family. Doubtless, part of this is due to Luke wanting to focus his narrative and not dilute it with too many extraneous stories. Nonetheless, Luke presents us with a pretty compelling picture of God using Peter in a unique and dynamic ministry, certainly different from that of the typical believer.

The next person who makes a dramatic impact is Stephen. One of the seven men chosen to serve the Hellenistic widows in food distribution, Stephen ended up having a powerful ministry which led to his being seized, brought before the Sanhedrin, and ultimately martyred. Since the apostles' rationale for choosing the seven was that "It would not be right for us to neglect the ministry of the word of God in order to wait on tables" (Acts 6:2), Stephen's example has sometimes been used to argue that God can do great things with "a simple waiter" if he's just willing to be used. However, the seven were chosen specifically because they were "full of the Spirit and wisdom" (Acts 6:3). Far from the contemporary penchant for throwing anyone who can do something into a slot for service, the apostles looked for people who were outstanding in terms of spirituality and insight, even for something that was, at least superficially, a mere menial and administrative task. So it should not be surprising that Stephen went on to be used in a greater way. He was the first non-apostle that Acts records as performing miracles, and he seems specifically to have had great wisdom in responding to opposition (Acts 6:8-10). His final defense of the Gospel in front of the Sanhedrin and his martyrdom were pivotal events in the life of the church, since they contributed to the disciples spreading the gospel to the surrounding area when they were scattered from Jerusalem, and because of the profound effect they had on a budding young rabbi named Saul who witnessed the event.

Philip, another of the seven, was responsible for the initial evangelizing of non-Jewish people, first in Samaria and then to the Ethiopian eunuch. In the persecution that erupted after the martyrdom of Stephen, Philip took the gospel to Samaria, where demonic deliverances and healings accompanied his gospel message, and many people believed and were baptized (Acts 8:5-13). It was when the apostles heard about the work that was already occurring in Stephen's ministry that Peter and John came to confirm it and to lay their hands on people to receive the Holy Spirit (vv. 14-17). Later, Philip traveled to a road that leads from Jerusalem to Gaza in response to an angelic message, and met an Ethiopian official, who was -probably one of the "God fearers," Gentiles who believed in the Jewish God but didn't officially convert to Judaism. (The Ethiopian would have been ineligible for conversion since he was a eunuch, according to Deuteronomy 23:1.) Philip explained the passage in Isaiah that the Ethiopian had been reading, shared with him the gospel of Jesus, and then baptized him. Subsequently, Philip made his way up the coast of the Mediterranean Sea from Azotus (historically, the Philistine city of Ashdod) to Caesarea, preaching the gospel all the way (Acts 8:26-40).

The last half of Acts is dominated by the Apostle Paul. Introduced at the scene of Stephen's stoning as Saul of

Tarsus, he was miraculously converted while on his way to Damascus, then almost immediately began preaching that Jesus was the Messiah (Acts 9:18-22). He had very little contact with the original apostles for many years (Galatians 1:15-2:2), during which time he had returned to his home town of Tarsus and from there was brought by Barnabas to work in the church in Antioch (Acts 11:25-26). His specific gifts were brought to the fore when he and Barnabas were set apart from among five leaders in Antioch and called on to begin spreading the gospel further west. Under opposition, Paul's gifts and personality came to the fore, and he became the dominant partner among his travelling companions from that point on (Acts 13:1-12). Paul endured tremendous physical and spiritual opposition for the next ten years or so, as he brought the gospel west into Turkey, Macedonia, and Greece, and then later, after he was arrested in Jerusalem, shared the gospel in Rome while living under house arrest. During his journeys and imprisonment, God also inspired him to write a number of letters that became a significant part of the New Testament canon.

Paul's story is compelling partly because of the tenacity with which he accomplished the work God set out for him to do. Clearly, God used someone with very particular gifts, abilities, and experiences—from his training as a rabbi in the Hebrew scriptures to his fanatical commitment to hunting down and arresting followers of Jesus, to his dramatic and miraculous conversion, blinding, and healing, to the impact that the stoning of Stephen had on him, which he spoke of years later as he recounted his conversion experience (Acts 22:20). Paul was, put bluntly, an irrepressible bulldog who felt compelled to preach the gospel (1 Cor. 9:16), possibly in response to his past persecution of Christians.

The point of recounting all of these stories of individuals in Acts is precisely that they *were* stories of individuals. Moreover, they are stories of just a few individuals over the course of about thirty years. They are strongly and very specifically gifted for definite types of ministry. Although there is no suggestion in Acts that these few people were the only people spreading the gospel in a systematic way, there is also no suggestion that they are simply representative of what was going on among the larger population of believers. Acts doesn't imply, in other words, that the gospel was spread primarily through an intentional effort among "ordinary" believers to evangelize their neighbors.

So this is the picture given to us by the book of Acts—the book that records what Jesus' disciples actually did in carrying out the Great Commission. On one hand, we have the character of the believers being demonstrated by sacrificial love toward one another and noticed by the surrounding populace; on the other, we have divinely-empowered leaders called and gifted for the task of spreading the gospel into new territory. Together, as a group, as a body, they accomplish Jesus' mission, each one doing his individual part. That's how outreach works, biblically. If we're going to use Acts as a model, that's what we see.

The Point of It All

One of the questions that the Christian faith has always claimed to answer is that of the nature and purpose of life. We are created to be in an eternal relationship with God; we have been torn apart from that relationship, and therefore from our own purpose, by our sin; God has sent Jesus in order to overcome the destruction our sin has caused and restore us to our original purpose.

While this explanation is valid as far as it goes, it has its limits. It is oriented (as is much in evangelical circles) toward the point of conversion. It explains why people have a need for God and what that need has to do with the question of purpose. It explains, in other words, why people should come to God in the first place, but not really what they should do once they get there. In other words, it satisfies the initial question of what life is all about, but then raises an additional question: What is the *Christian* life all about?

This is not a mere academic question. It's a common experience for people to come to Jesus, perhaps even with a radical conversion experience, have an initial period of excitement, fulfillment, and wonder at their newfound life, only at some point months or perhaps a year or two down the line to begin wondering, "Now what?"

The typical answer to that question is evangelism. It is sometimes even stated straight out from the pulpit: "The only reason you continue to live on Planet Earth after you get saved is to bring as many people as possible with you to heaven." So that's the idea: your purpose is to have a relationship with God through Jesus, and you've accomplished that by getting saved; now your purpose is to help as many other people achieve their purposes as possible. Given that God's love for people should motivate us to love them as well, this seems to be a natural progression. Unfortunately, it also seems to run afoul both of personal experience and of biblical warrant. While most new believers are eager to share their experience with Christ when it's fresh, this motivation seems to wane right around the time they begin asking the question of "Now what?" It would seem that if personal evangelism were the answer to the question, then the natural evangelistic efforts of new believers would be self-sustaining—we would be continually renewed and motivated by the very actions that are so natural upon conversion. Instead, we find that after some period of time, most (not all) new believers have to be encouraged in keeping up their outreach efforts. This is generally attributed to loss of first love, the opposition of Satan, an apathetic church culture, or any number of other reasons. Essentially, it is understood that something is wrong, and what is wrong is not the model but the participants.

If this were the case, one would expect to see evidence of it in Scripture. That is to say, one would expect to see personal evangelism as a significant component of what the new life looks like (as the major reason for existence that already-converted believers have), and one would expect to see believers who are struggling with spiritual opposition or apathy being encouraged to reach out to those who have not yet come to faith. Oddly enough, this is just what one does not find.

As detailed in the previous chapter, the book of Acts, which is where one would expect to find strong positive evidence for personal evangelism among ordinary believers, actually describes in a few passages a community of people whose behavior toward one another influences many people to join the movement, and in the rest of the book, describes the missionary achievements of a few supernaturally-empowered individual believers. Rather than those believers simply representing Christians in general, Acts gives the distinct impression that each one is uniquely called to accomplish the work that he in fact accomplishes.

But Acts, it may be argued, is simply about these specific missionary efforts. It leaves the role of personal evangelism out (or largely out) simply because that's not what the story is about. And that may be the case. But one would also expect to read a great deal about overt outreach in the epistles as well. As letters written to address problems and difficulties—or even simply to encourage what is going well—the epistles must have included a plethora of encouragement, instruction, and correction in the area of sharing the gospel with those around us. In fact, they don't.

Most of the epistles are divided into a largely doctrinal section and a largely practical section. In the book of Romans, for example, the first eleven chapters are primarily doctrinal, while chapters 12 through 15 are largely practical. (Chapter 16 is comprised of personal greetings.) Some books, such as 1 Corinthians and James, are almost entirely practical in nature. The sections of the epistles that are more practical in nature are called the paranetic sections of the epistles, and this is where we would expect to find practical instruction or correction regarding evangelism.

In Romans, for example, chapter 12 deals with general Christian character, including encouragement to serve faithfully in one's gifts. Verse 11 warns against lacking in zeal, but applies this imperative to serving the Lord, not (at least not explicitly) to sharing one's faith. Verses 17-21 involve the believing reader's relationship with "everyone," so this clearly involves relationships with unbelievers, but Paul discusses living at peace with others and responding to evil, not evangelism. Chapter 13 involves one's relationship with governing authorities, living in love, and living in purity because of our impending salvation.

Romans 14 deals with different believers having different convictions regarding "disputable matters." Romans 15 concludes this discussion, exhorting believers to bear with one another, after which Paul begins describing his role as God's minister to the Gentiles. Verse 16 does discuss preaching the gospel, but refers specifically to Paul's own preaching. The end of the chapter refers to Paul's intention to visit Rome on his way to Spain.

So the paranetic section of Romans, although it deals with many issues, from relationships with the world outside the Christian fellowship to warnings against drunkenness and debauchery, has nothing to say, either by way of encouragement, teaching, or rebuke, on the duty of believers to share their faith with others.

Let's try another book: Ephesians. Ephesians is split pretty evenly in half: chapters 1-3 are doctrinal in nature, chapters 4-6 are practical. The practical section begins with a plea for unity and maturity among believers. Paul then appeals to his readers to live lives of truthfulness, honesty, compassion, and forgiveness, in contrast to the sensuality, greed, bitterness, and conflict exhibited among the unbelieving Gentiles. In chapter 5, Paul continues to exhort his readers to lives of character befitting the "children of light" that they now are. He then turns to specific relationships: husbands and wives, children and parents, slaves and masters. In each case, he balances the expected counsel of humble submission on the part of culturally subordinate partners (wives, children, slaves) with novel advice to the culturally dominant partners (husbands, parents, masters) of moderating the use of their authority and using it for the good of all involved, not just their own.

Paul concludes with the metaphor of the armor of God, once again focusing on attributes of character and spirituality in picturing a battle between the believer and the "powers of this dark world," and finally exhorts his readers toward prayer. Here he does mention preaching the gospel, but does so in the context of his readers praying that he, Paul, would "declare it fearlessly." So once again, we have no practical teaching on sharing one's faith in the book of Ephesians.

Were we to continue this survey, we would find that this is the pattern throughout the epistles. There is a great deal of exhortation for believers to exhibit the kind of character and lifestyle that are worthy of emulation, reflect well on Jesus and the gospel, promote loving and peaceful relationships both within and outside the fellowship of believers, and encourage one's individual spiritual growth. This is complemented by warnings to leave behind the kind of dissolute lifestyle that many of the believers evidently had lived up to the point of their conversion, and to which some were returning, and from which others had perhaps never completely disengaged. There are appeals to pray and to have fellowship with one another. By contrast, teaching on individuals sharing their faith is noticeably absent. In fact, one gets the strong impression that godly character, lived out in the marketplace of the world at large, is itself the witness that most believers are expected to exhibit, which supports the work done by those who are especially gifted and called to evangelism and missionary endeavors.

Lest one think that I have simply chosen examples in which evangelism was not prominent and then asserted by fiat that the rest of the epistles conform to that pattern, let's try a more systematic approach, examining words that relate to evangelism and outreach. *Euangelizo* ("preach the gospel") is used almost exclusively in Paul's epistles to refer to his own preaching. He also uses it to refer to hypothetical examples (Rom. 10:15, "how can anyone preach unless they are sent?"; Gal. 1:8-9, "If anybody is preaching to you a gospel other than what you accepted"), to Jesus' preaching (Eph. 2:17), and to Timothy bringing good news (1 Thess. 3:6). In the general epistles, it is used in the passive to refer to the gospel being preached to those who are now believers (Heb. 4:2, 6; 1 Pet. 1:12, 25; 4:6).[3]

In its noun form, *euangelion* ("gospel") generally refers to the content of the gospel message, or occasionally to the time period since the Resurrection during which the gospel has been preached, or to the growing Christian movement itself. Preaching or sharing the gospel is sometimes expressed in this form as well, but always with reference to Paul or other apostles and evangelists (e.g., Eph. 6:19, 1 Thess. 2:2, 8). There is no support for a universal evangelistic obligation found in these references.[4]

The verb *kerusso* ("preach" or "proclaim"), in constructions like "preach Christ," is sometimes used in place of *euangelizo*. It generally either has as its explicit or implied

---

[3] *Euangelizo* in the epistles: Rom. 1:15; 10:15; 15:20; 1Co. 1:17; 9:16, 18; 1Co. 15:1; 1-2; 2Co. 10:16; 11:7; Gal. 1:8-9, 11, 16, 23; 4:13; Eph. 2:17; 3:8; 1Th. 3:6; Heb. 4:2, 6; 1Pe. 1:12, 25; 4:6.

[4] *Euangelion* in the epistles: Rom. 1:1,9,16; 2:16; 10:16; 11:28; 15:16,19,29; 16:25; 1Co. 4:15; 9:12,14,18,23; 15:1; 2Co. 2:12; 4:3,4; 8:18; 9:13; 10:14; 11:4,7; Gal. 1:6,7,11; 2:2,5,7,14; Eph. 1:13; 3:6; 6:15,19; Php. 1:5,7,12,17,27; 2:22; 4:3,15; Col. 1:5,23; 1Th. 1:5; 2:2,4,8,9; 3:2; 2Th. 1:8; 2:14; 1Ti. 1:11; 2Ti. 1:8,10; 2:8; Phm. 1:13; 1Pe. 4:17.

subject Paul, his traveling companions, or the other apostles, or else the subject is left undefined because the point of the passage is about what has been preached or those who have heard the preaching. It never makes reference to typical believers preaching or being expected or encouraged to preach.[5]

It is used, however, in one passage that is germane to the subject and is well-known and often quoted:

"Everyone who calls on the name of the Lord will be saved."

How, then, can they call on the one they have not believed in? And how can they believe in the one of whom they have not heard? And how can they hear without someone preaching to them? And how can anyone preach unless they are sent? As it is written: "How beautiful are the feet of those who bring good news!"

Romans 10:13-15

This passage ties salvation with calling on the name of the Lord, calling on the name with faith, and faith with the preaching of the gospel message. It thus provides impetus to the mission of reaching unreached people, and often forms part of an appeal for believers in general to share their faith with others.

But in context, the passage forms a part of Paul's contrast between "righteousness that is by the law" and "righteousness that is by faith" (Rom. 10:5-6), insisting

---

[5] *Kerusso* in the epistles: Rom. 2:21; 10:8,14,15; 1Co. 1:23; 9:27; 15:11,12; 2Co. 1:19; 4:5; 11:4; Gal. 2:2; 5:11; Php. 1:15; Col. 1:23; 1Th. 2:9; 1Ti. 3:16; 2Ti. 4:2; 1Pe. 3:19.

that salvation comes only through the latter, even for Jews, and that the Hebrew scriptures themselves pointed to this development (verse 13 is a quote from Joel 2:32). Moreover, the final link in Paul's chain of reasoning is that those who preach must be "sent," probably a not-so-subtle appeal for support of his own missionary efforts and his desire to take the gospel as far as Spain (Rom. 15:24, 28). At any rate, the necessity of being "sent" seems to indicate a more formal means of proclamation than simply people sharing their faith. It would also indicate that those doing the "sending"—i.e., supporting evangelistic work indirectly through prayer, financial support, and encouragement—might have as much a part to play in bringing people to saving faith as those who actually do the preaching. Once again, different people using a variety of gifts actually accomplish the work.

But perhaps the terms we've been searching for are too formalized themselves. One may argue that only a certain segment of believers are called upon to "preach the gospel," but we are all called to be "witnesses" (Acts 1:8). However, this approach still does not prove to be fruitful. The noun form *martus* ("witness") is never used in Scripture to mean one who shares one's faith with an unbeliever. It is most often used in its ordinary sense as a legal term referring to one who has seen, or witnessed, an event. Paul frequently uses it in the formula "God is my witness," to affirm his truthfulness. In some cases, he calls upon his readers as witnesses to his character. Peter refers to himself as "a witness of Christ's sufferings"

(1 Pet. 5:1).[6] Similarly, the verb form *martureo* ("to witness") is used in the passive to refer to people "of good report," that is, having a positive reputation. Paul often uses it of himself, affirming that something positive is true about his readers. But once again, the verb is never used in the modern sense of "witnessing"—i.e., intentionally going out to share the gospel, or one's own personal experience in Christ, with those who are not yet believers.[7]

So Acts and the New Testament epistles don't offer the kind of support one would expect to find if evangelism on the part of every believer individually was God's expectation and was as central to the Christian life as the evangelical church teaches. In truth, that should make the case definitively. If the history of the church and the letters God inspired to be written to the church do not affirm evangelical doctrine at this point, then that evangelical doctrine is, at best, a secondary point to be inferred from indirect scriptural evidence.

Some may say that evidence from the Gospels is being ignored. Clearly Jesus proclaimed the gospel of the Kingdom; clearly he chose others (first the twelve, then the seventy) to do the same; he told them that they would do the same things that he had been doing, and even greater things (John 14:12); his final message to his disciples,

---

[6] *Martus* in the epistles: Mat. 18:16; 26:65; Mark 14:63; Luke 24:48; Acts 1:8,22; 2:32; 3:15; 5:32; 6:13; 7:58; 10:39,41; 13:31; 22:15,20; 26:16; Rom. 1:9; 2Co. 1:23; 13:1; Php. 1:8; 1Th. 2:5,10; 1Ti. 5:19; 6:12; 2Ti. 2:2; Heb. 10:28; 12:1; 1Pe. 5:1.

[7] *Martureo* in the epistles: Acts 6:3; 10:22,43; 13:22; 14:3; 15:8; 16:2; 22:5,12; 23:11; 26:5,22; Rom. 3:21; 10:2; 1Co. 15:15; 2Co. 8:3; Gal. 4:15; Col. 4:13; 1Th. 2:11; 1Ti. 5:10; 6:13; Heb. 7:8,17; 10:15; 11:2,4,5,39; 1Jn. 1:2; 4:14; 5:6,7,8,9,10; 3Jn. 1:3,6,12.

according to Matthew, was that they make disciples of all nations. It couldn't be more obvious that Jesus was setting up a mandate for us to continue on with his work once he had physically left this world.

But this ignores the fact that Acts and the epistles are themselves the record of how the disciples did in fact carry on with that mission after Jesus' ascension. They reveal how those who had actually lived and spoken with Jesus, those who were in the best position to know what it was that he expected them to do going forward, actually did in response to that challenge. And as we've seen, what they did was not impose a universal obligation of outreach on every believer, but rather focus on encouraging believers to live out lives of exemplary character among the unbelieving world, and empower specific gifted individuals to do overt outreach.

One can see that in some ways this is what Jesus did. At first, he simply preaches the message of the Kingdom, exemplified in the Sermon on the Mount, which itself focuses on character and ethics; later, he chooses from among the crowds that were following him a dozen particular individuals to work with and train. These he did send out two by two to do the same things he had been doing (Matthew 10)—preaching the message of the Kingdom, as well as casting out demons and healing the sick. Later he sent seventy (or seventy-two[8]; Luke 10) to do the same thing. So one may see a geometric progression of

---

[8] Manuscripts are divided on whether the number was seventy or seventy-two, and translations and experts in textual criticism are also divided. Kurt Aland prefers seventy-two; Bruce Metzger prefers seventy.

disciples going out to spread the word of the Kingdom. The evangelical church would argue that the ongoing mission to reach the lost is simply an extension of that progression.

However, the commissioning of the seventy only appears in the Gospel of Luke (by contrast with the commissioning of the twelve, which appears in all three Synoptics), so the idea of a geometric progression is not something that scripture invests with significant emphasis. The gospels were originally written as standalone documents; in three out of four of them, this progression isn't even present. The most we can say is that Jesus did first send out the twelve and then the seventy; whether he intended a geometric progression to occur in the same way after his resurrection is at best a matter of conjecture. We don't see confirmation of it in Acts; there is not, for example, a mission of the 120 who were in the upper room on the day of Pentecost.

This raises the most significant issue with regard to looking at the gospels and at Jesus' earthly ministry as a model for ministry today: it ignores all the probable differences between the proclamation of the Kingdom that John the Baptist and Jesus were engaged in, and the post-resurrection message of salvation. Certainly they are related—the Kingdom that was "at hand" turned out to be inaugurated by the salvation and lordship of the risen Christ in the lives of those who trust in him. But there are distinctions. Paul found disciples in Ephesus who had been baptized under John's baptism and hadn't heard of the Holy Spirit, and judged that they needed baptism again, and the coming of the Holy Spirit on them when they were baptized seems to indicate that Paul was right (Acts 19:1-7). This was John's baptism and not that of Jesus, but we still don't know exactly what the baptism that Jesus' disciples were performing consisted of (John 4:2)—that is to say, was it already the fully Christian baptism in the name of the Father, Son, and Holy Spirit? It seems more likely that during that time it was also simply a baptism of repentance. So even those who were baptized by Jesus' disciples during his earthly ministry probably needed some sort of further development— possibly including another baptism—to become fully-Christian believers in the post-resurrection sense. What we are doing, after Jesus' resurrection, is not simply a contin- uation of Jesus' earthly ministry.

My point is not to make a hard dispensational distinc- tion between Jesus' earthly ministry and the post- resurrection Christian ministry that followed, which would make Jesus' life and ministry all-but-irrelevant to us in the "church age." My point is rather to suggest that the earthly ministry of Jesus was not and could not possibly have been exactly the sort of thing that the disciples did after Jesus' resurrection, or what we should be engaged in today. Some contemporary teaching seems to view Jesus in the same way one would view any other leader starting a movement, with the role of later generations of follow- ers being simply to pass on his teachings and his methods after he is gone. But this doesn't take into account the resurrection, the climactic point of all the gospels. The resurrection changed everything, which is why it becomes the focus of every sermon preached in Acts. What Jesus said about eating his flesh and drinking his blood appeared merely bizarre until his death and resurrection gave it context. So to pattern present-day ministry after Jesus' earthly ministry without thinking through the differences that the resurrection made is to follow a faulty example. Examining the way Jesus performed miracles, we can see that he often performed the same miracle in several different ways. He seems to be making a point out of us *not* applying a formula. His message was not, "Follow my methodology," but rather, "Follow me."

So to sum up: the evangelical church asserts a biblical mandate for all believers to be involved in some sort of evangelism or outreach to those who do not yet believe. But when we search the scriptures, we find little evidence to support this mandate. Jesus' ministry as recorded in the gospels was at least in some sense unique, and Acts and the epistles demonstrate how the directive to "make disciples" actually played out in the decades immediately following Jesus' resurrection. Acts shows us, not every believer reaching out to all of his or her friends and neighbors with the gospel, but rather living out the implications of that gospel in their practical love and care for one another, and a number of especially gifted individuals who were called specifically to do mission work and evangelize those who did not yet believe. The epistles give us plenty of instruction on godly living and character, with explicit implications drawn regarding the effect that this lifestyle would have on unbelievers, but there is practically nothing in terms of command, encouragement, instruction, or rebuke regarding evangelism or outreach.

I'm sure that this drawn-out attack on the idea of an evangelical obligation on all believers is painful, grieving, or angering to many. Why would someone professing faith in Jesus argue so stridently against sharing that faith with others? Why are we even talking in terms of obligation? Isn't there a heartfelt desire to see people saved? What kind of a monster wants to see people go to hell?

Once again, my point is not that evangelism shouldn't happen or isn't important. It's not to encourage a cavalier disregard for people's salvation. It is simply to suggest that God himself may not have designed the gospel to spread in that manner, and may not have designed all of us to be able to function as outgoing soul-winners. It may be that our model of how evangelism is supposed to work is deficient, that we might be able to view it in a different light, and that viewing it in a different light might encourage, rather than discourage, more believers' participation in the larger advancement of the Kingdom that will result in the salvation of those who do not at this point believe.

The typical model of how evangelism is supposed to work divides people into two categories, Saved and Lost. These categories are completely distinct and separate from one another. Every individual is in one category or the other. No one can be in both, or anywhere in between. This view could be illustrated like this:

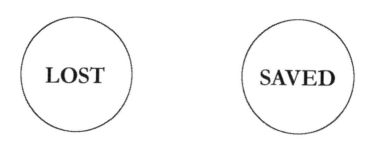

There might be secondary differences within each category—among the Lost might be those who are apathetic to the gospel, those who are actively hostile, those who are devoted to other religions, and those who are atheists and have no supernatural beliefs at all; among the Saved might be those who are new converts and need instruction, those who are strongly committed and growing, those who are relatively apathetic, and those who are enthusiastically "on fire." But these divisions are considered more or less intramural and aren't really connected with the overarching goal of evangelism. The only distinctions made would be in relation to technique—how one goes about trying to reach a particular group from among the Lost—or impetus—how one goes about trying to motivate those from among the Saved to do evangelism in the first place.

It should be noted that there is some biblical support for this sort of dichotomous view. As in the parable of the Sheep and the Goats, Jesus and the biblical writers often categorize people in just these sorts of terms, and after the Last Judgment, all people will be either in God's kingdom or out of it. Whatever may be found to be the defects of viewing humanity exclusively by this model, it must be admitted that it is at least one valid perspective.

So according to this model, from the point of view of the Saved, the primary relationship that should exist between themselves and the Lost would be characterized as outreach. Any friendships, acquaintances, business relationships, associations, and the like that may exist are ultimately there to serve the purpose of outreach. God put that person into your life in order for you to be a witness to him or to her. You are in that job, you are in that club, you are in that neighborhood for the express purpose of being salt and light to the people who are there. And to the extent that you don't have associations with the Lost, you should intentionally cultivate them in order to find means of reaching out to them.

The goal of all this outreach is to produce the result of Conversion. We want to bring people from the category of the Lost into the category of the Saved. This conversion process is accompanied by various sorts of indicators: recital of a sinner's prayer, response to an altar call, overtly and publicly making a decision for Christ, renouncing past sins and expressing repentance, identification with and participation in a faith community. So our diagram could be expanded to reflect these interactions between the two basic groups:

Outreach

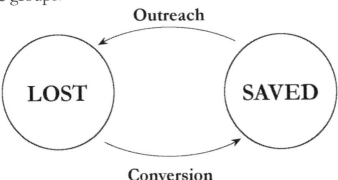

LOST   **SAVED**

Conversion

Once again, there is biblical support for this model. Jesus and Peter and Philip and Paul and many others do engage in overt outreach to get the message of the gospel out to those who are unbelievers; people like Zacchaeus and the Philippian jailer have clear and overt conversion experiences. To some degree, at least, this model describes exactly what the church's mission is, and I would not want to be thought to minimize it.

Nonetheless, this model also seems to be a bit reductionistic. As earlier noted, it fails to take into account varying degrees and varieties of Saved and Lost people. It also fails to take into account the fact that, at least on the level of our own human perceptions of one another, the division between saved and lost can sometimes seem less of an absolute gulf than a sometimes blurry line. God certainly knows the heart of the apathetic churchgoer, as well as the non-churchgoer who has a longing for God but has been hurt by organized religion in the past. As human onlookers, however, we don't. Even the self-perception of people in both categories can be faulty: some people falsely believe themselves to be saved (or without a need to be saved); some people have a faith relationship with Jesus but struggle with wondering whether they are actually saved or not. Any pastor has dealt with many people of both categories. God certainly knows where each person is, but it may be that in his wisdom, our categories don't actually make sense. We might ask, "If you were to die tonight, where would you go?" but since God may know that that person is not, in fact, going to die for the next twenty years, the question of where that person would go at any particular point in time is moot. That person may be in a God-ordained process going from darkness to light; the question of what point in time, exactly, that person went from a state of being Lost to one of being Saved might possibly be meaningless. Even if it's not meaningless, it is hidden to us humans.

So another way to look at human beings might be that of a spectrum, instead of two discrete categories. There might be varying degrees of unbelief and belief, ranging from outright hostility or indifference to the gospel on one end to fervent and growing spirituality on the other. The range might look something like this:

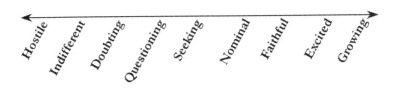

LOST   SAVED

It should be clear that this model, in its own way, is just as deficient as the distinct Saved-Lost model. It's difficult to assess whether being hostile or indifferent is further away from the Saved side of the spectrum, and sometimes people who are outwardly the most hostile to the gospel are in fact closer to a dramatic conversion than those who appear to be seeking—Saul of Tarsus comes to mind, by contrast with Simon the Sorcerer (Acts 8:9-24). Moreover, if we view people's spiritual journeys as traversing the spectrum from left to right (or perhaps the reverse), we can see that people seldom make the kinds of smooth transitions that the spectrum may suggest—few people, when converted, slide from being seeking unbelievers to nominal believers. When someone is converted, they generally go a lot further than that; the nominal believer is often someone who has been a professing Christian for some time but has stopped growing and has become stagnant. But despite its limitations, the spectrum can be nonetheless useful in recognizing another means by which evangelism can occur.

Let's imagine George, a person with a rough past who was saved as an adult through a dramatic conversion experience. That person has a great deal of life experience as someone who was unbelieving, even hostile to the gospel. Besides a newfound zeal for Jesus and for reaching other people for him, George has something else that is invaluable with regard to outreach: a deep understanding of how someone thinks as an unbeliever, the doubts that unbelievers may have, the types of intellectual, emotional, and relational inroads that made it possible to come from a life of unbelief to faith. George also knows the language, the mannerisms, and the environment in which he used to live, and has a certain comfort level in that environment. There may be a period of time after conversion during which George might need to stay out of his previous surroundings, in order not to relapse into former patterns of sin. But once George is fully grounded, he may be able to move within that milieu and reach people in a way that someone without that life experience may not. The range on the spectrum that encompasses George's life experiences, from hostility to the gospel to present-day experience, might be represented on the spectrum in this way:

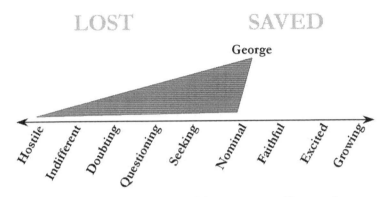

The shaded triangle would represent George's area of influence, the region in which he might be able to reach out to others effectively, based on the life experience that allows him to connect with others in those areas of the spectrum. The object would always be to draw people from wherever they are on the spectrum toward the right hand side, closer and closer to a deep relationship with Jesus. The bottom of the triangle ends on the right hand side where it does because it is generally impossible for someone to help draw someone else further toward Jesus than the person doing the drawing already has come. There are exceptions, but that's generally the rule.

George may well be an excellent evangelist. Having covered the spectrum, he should be able to reach out effectively to many people on the Lost side. It is important to note that this effectiveness is not merely a function of what George is personally comfortable with; it is mostly a function of the people who are likely to be comfortable associating with a person like George. Those who don't know the language, the mannerisms, and the environment of the people that they are trying to reach are highly unlikely to be able to reach them with any effectiveness, no matter how willing or passionate they are. This is one of the first things that those who do missionary work are taught. This is what the Apostle Paul meant when he said that he became "all things to all people" in order to reach them where they were (1 Cor. 9:19-23). The more like you I am, the more you are likely to be willing to listen to what I have to say (assuming, of course, that I am being like you in ways that don't compromise my message). Missionaries sometimes spend years learning the language, culture, and customs of the people they are going to attempt to reach; native converts don't have that hurdle to cross. Someone who comes to faith from an unbelieving subculture has exactly the same advantages when trying to reach back into that subculture.

Now consider Grace, a person who grew up in a Christian home, made a commitment to Jesus at an early age, never rebelled in a significant way, and whose life experiences are largely bounded by the Church. Grace is going to be able to reach a different segment of the spectrum in a different way:

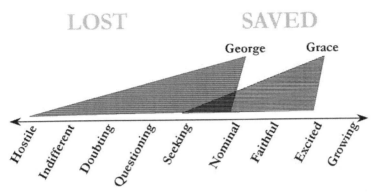

Grace is not going to have the background that will give her a rapport with people who are significantly distanced from Christian circles. However, there are people that she can influence in a godly direction, from people who might just be seeking, to people who are nominal believers, to those who are faithful but not deeply excited or growing in their faith. Grace might help develop someone who has just come to faith or rescue someone who is sliding away from a formerly zealous relationship with Jesus. She can be an invaluable help within the body of Christ, and accomplish things that George couldn't.

But on the original model, where the Saved and the Lost are considered as two very separate, discrete categories, only George is truly accomplishing his purpose of outreach to the lost. Grace might do a bit of evangelism when the opportunity arises with someone who is genuinely searching, but in general, Grace's most natural venue of ministry is going to be locked within the Saved circle. In an environment where outreach to the Lost is the only thing that truly matters, Grace's most natural area of ministry is subtly invalidated.

All of this, of course, refers to the typical and natural areas of influence that most believers will operate in. It has nothing to do with supernatural empowerments that God may give to an individual believer. God empowered a deeply zealous Jew named Saul to become the most influential early apostle to the Gentiles. In recent times, he used a sheltered rural Pennsylvania pastor named David Wilkerson to reach out to hardened street gangs in urban New York. God can and does use any number of people to reach various sorts of other people in many unexpected ways, and it's often suggested, subtly or otherwise, that those who don't reach out much to unbelievers lack either the faith or the willingness to be drawn out of their "comfort zone." But what this does, in those situations where a person is not specially gifted or called for such an unusual form of ministry, is to discourage believers from doing what they would naturally be good at and channel their efforts into avenues of ministry that are frustrating and unfulfilling to them.

When George and Grace are both allowed to focus on their most natural areas of influence, an interesting thing happens. As a relatively new believer, George is in Grace's area of influence. As Grace uses her influence to help George develop in his faith, George's own passion for God continues to grow. He is enabled to minister to his own area of influence more effectively, as he understands his faith and lives it out better. Since his area of influence includes many unbelievers, some of them may come to faith. Grace will continue to grow in her own faith as she continues to use her gifts; George will continue to grow and begin to be able to mentor younger believers, including Gary, who came to Jesus by means of George's influence, and who now has his own area of influence. This creates a current effect, in which each person draws the next person toward the right side of the spectrum.

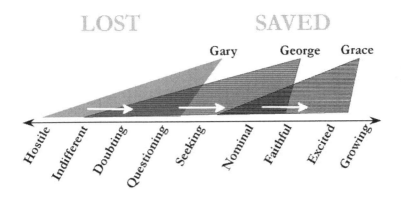

Discipling younger believers has the overall effect of bringing new people into the "saved" region—possibly a greater effect than if someone like Grace were to try to directly witness to those who are still unbelievers.

All this relates to the original question posed by this chapter. What is the purpose of the Christian life? Aside from having our sins forgiven and going to heaven when we die, what exactly are we doing here? The typical evangelical response is evangelism. We are here to bring other people to Jesus, to save other people from hell. For those who have a calling toward it, that view is fulfilling and self-evident. What could be better than sharing with others what we ourselves have received?

But for many—probably most—who do not have a clear calling to evangelism, the answer is a bit more complicated. The purpose of life is to exercise whatever gifts and talents God has given, to do our best with who we are, to worship God and serve others, and by doing so, to be a part of accomplishing God's larger purpose, which involves redeeming both a people and a world, restoring both to the pristine state they should have had before sin corrupted and distorted it. That is, individual people living out the individual purposes dictated by their individual gifts work together, not only to bring as many people as possible to Christ, but to help them to become as much like Christ as possible. Maybe your effect on others is to draw them to being willing to listen to the gospel. Maybe you effectively deliver the gospel to those who have been so prepared. Maybe you take people who already know the gospel and bring them to the next level of maturity and obedience. "I planted the seed, Apollos watered it, but God has been making it grow" (1 Cor. 3:6).

That's the answer. In Christ, you get to be yourself, only better. You get to be the you that you could never be, maybe the you that you could never even envision. You get to be the best you imaginable. But it's you, not the prefab cookie cutout that someone else, however well intentioned, thought you should be. It's the you that your creator thought you should be, actually created you to be, to perform the part in the great drama that could only be fulfilled by you.

Spiritual Gifts

Throughout this discussion, the issue of spiritual gift-edness has been a common theme, even though historical-ly they've been neglected or distorted by the church as a whole. This, in a way, is odd, because one of the most frequent images we use to describe the church is that of the body. We refer to the church as the body of Christ much more often than we do other metaphors that the Bible uses, such as bride of Christ or God's temple. What we've missed is that the metaphor of the body is used only in a few places in the New Testament, and in all of the places where that analogy is fleshed out with some detail, we find that it is used with reference to spiritual gifts. Let's look at the passages:

> For by the grace given me I say to every one of you: Do not think of yourself more highly than you ought, but rather think of yourself with sober judgment, in accordance with the faith God has distributed to each of you. For just as each of us has one body with many members, and these members do not all have the same function, so in Christ we, though many, form one body, and each member belongs to all the others. We have

different gifts, according to the grace given to each of us. If your gift is prophesying, then prophesy in accordance with your faith; if it is serving, then serve; if it is teaching, then teach; if it is to encourage, then give encouragement; if it is giving, then give generously; if it is to lead, do it diligently; if it is to show mercy, do it cheerfully.

Romans 12:3-7

Here we see that the point that Paul made by using the analogy of the body is not simply that we are all a part of one unit—which is how most people understand it—but that we are a part of one body with many members. What Paul emphasizes is the separate functions of the various members of the body. The point is twofold: "Each member belongs to all the others"—so there must be unity; but also, "We have different gifts, according to the grace given to each of us."—there must be diversity. Unity with diversity: that's the message. Not only unity with diversity: unity through diversity, perhaps even unity because of diversity, unity dependent upon diversity. The people of God are like the different members (we would probably say, "organs") of the human body, not at all like pennies in a roll or cookies cut from the same cookie cutter. Not only *are* we different, we are *supposed* to be different, we are created to be different, we are given grace (as the scripture explicitly states) to be different. [9]

---

[9] Many of the insights in this chapter I owe to C. Peter Wagner, from *Your Spiritual Gifts Can Help Your Church Grow.* Updated and Expanded ed. Ventura, CA: Regal Books, 2012. Print.

Not many people would explicitly oppose this. We make fun of the idea of "cookie-cutter Christians." But our practices demonstrate how little we truly understand and apply this approach practically. Almost everything we encourage people to do in the Christian life we think everyone should do, pretty much in the same measure. Pray, read the Bible, witness, attend church, follow certain external social conventions (internal sins we're allowed to "struggle" with), perhaps get involved in a small group fellowship; all these things are things we encourage every believer to do. If we make any distinctions at all, we make distinctions between leadership and "ordinary" believers; and the main distinction we make here is one of quantity: we think that our leaders should do more of these things, not necessarily different things or the same things in a different way. We might make distinctions involving talent, which does swerve close to the idea of spiritual gifts (properly understood), but these distinctions are generally limited to skills relating to public ministry, such as musical or speaking ability. We might allow one another to have different sorts of personalities, but we expect one another to be essentially the same sort of Christian.

This is not at all the vision that Paul describes as that of the Body. For Paul, God graciously grants each believer various types of spiritual gifts to be used for one another's benefit and to one coordinated purpose—each one "belongs to all the others." That's the unity part. But each gift is different, and each person is encouraged to pursue and use the gift that he or she has been granted—not to try to obtain someone else's gift or what someone decides is a more important gift. Once we've understood that we're all to be working together for one goal, the scripture sets us free to pursue whatever it is that God has given to each one of us.

The gifts listed in this passage are prophecy, serving, teaching, encouragement, giving, leadership, and mercy. A few things should be noticed here. Nothing in the passage suggests that this list is exhaustive, and as we will see, in the various passages where Paul talks about spiritual gifts, he has a different list.[10] The lists overlap, but none are exactly the same as the others, even at the beginning and end of 1 Corinthians 12. It seems clear that all of these lists are intended to be not exhaustive, but rather representative—Paul has selected them from among all the various conceivable gifts because they apply to the people and situations he is addressing in each context. Probably, even if we were to combine all the various lists into one, that "master list" would still not necessarily be exhaustive. There might be other gifts that Paul does not explicitly name as a gift. His point is for us to recognize the various types of things that God has given in different measures to different believers so that we may all rely on one another for the good of the Kingdom.

It's also unwarranted to take each of these lists and set them apart as a different type of gift (as some have done) so that, for instance, the list in Romans 12 is thought of as being "personality" gifts, the ones in 1 Corinthians 12 as

---

[10] The analogy of the Body and spiritual gifts seem to be one of Paul's unique contributions to the New Testament writings. None of the other biblical writers use this terminology.

"sign" or "miraculous" gifts, and the ones in Ephesians 4 as "ministry" gifts. Nothing in their respective contexts identifies or categorizes them in this way. More than likely, the different gift lists Paul comes up with in letters to different churches are determined by the situations he is responding to in each of these different contexts.

But regarding the gifts Paul lists specifically in Romans 12, it will be seen at once that most of them are not obviously miraculous or supernatural in nature. While many who teach and write on spiritual gifts insist that these gifts are to be considered as completely separate from natural talents and abilities, it is unclear why this should be the case. Separating "natural" talents and abilities from "spiritual" gifts makes an unnecessary division—it presupposes that what we think of as "natural" is somehow of a different order than what we think of as "spiritual," that one is intrinsic to us while the other is bestowed from outside ourselves. In fact, both must be seen as graciously given to us by God. One of our greatest acts of pride is taking credit for what we seem innately to be good at, instead of acknowledging that everything good we have comes from God. As Paul writes to the Corinthians, "Who makes you different from anyone else? What do you have that you did not receive? And if you did receive it, why do you boast as though you did not?" (1 Cor. 4:7) Once we understand Paul's point here, the difference between what we think we possess naturally and what we recognize to be a gift disappears: it's all been given to us by God.

To be certain, some gifts will be outgrowths of what we've had a natural talent for since childhood; other gifts will be skills that we have developed over the course of study, time, and practice; still other gifts may be bestowed by more obviously supernatural means—things that were at one time weaknesses for us, things that we have not studied or practiced into learned skills, things which no amount of study or practice could have made into a skill, but which at a certain point God simply enables us to do. For us to have a healthy understanding of what Paul means by our status as members of one body, we must recognize that not only those things which have obviously been given to us as gifts, but everything that we have and are, is a gift from God and is to be used in his service and to the benefit of the Body as a whole.

So Paul encourages each of his readers in Rome to pursue those gifts which are already evident in their lives. A reader might reasonably wonder why it would be necessary for Paul to encourage them to do that. Isn't that the natural thing that they would want to do, independent of any encouragement? In general, the answer would be yes, but this is where Paul's introduction to the passage plays a part. His initial appeal is for each of his readers not to "think of yourself more highly than you ought", which then leads into the discussion of the members of the body and the various spiritual gifts that people possess. The connection to be made here, which is made more explicitly in 1 Corinthians 12, is that our sinful human reasoning doesn't naturally lend itself to the idea of various gifts that coexist and are interdependent. We tend to want to magnify what we happen to be good at and passionate about, not recognizing that we represent only a part of the big picture, that God wants us to be passionate about the things he's given to us as gifts, while allowing others to be just as passionate about the things he's given to them. The instruction for each of us to pursue our own gifts whole-heartedly is also an instruction for us to allow others room to pursue their own gifts just as unreservedly.

This balance between recognizing and pursuing our own gifts and giving room for others to do the same is the primary focus of the second main gift passage from 1 Corinthians 12. Although it is a long passage to quote, it seems worthwhile to do so, since there are so many aspects of it that invite our interaction:

> There are different kinds of gifts, but the same Spirit distributes them. There are different kinds of service, but the same Lord. There are different kinds of working, but in all of them and in every-one it is the same God at work.
>
> Now to each one the manifestation of the Spirit is given for the common good. To one there is given through the Spirit a message of wisdom, to another a message of knowledge by means of the same Spirit, to another faith by the same Spirit, to another gifts of healing by that one Spirit, to another miraculous powers, to an-other prophecy, to another distinguishing be-tween spirits, to another speaking in different kinds of tongues, and to still another the interpre-tation of tongues. All these are the work of one and the same Spirit, and he distributes them to each one, just as he determines.

Just as a body, though one, has many parts, but all its many parts form one body, so it is with Christ. For we were all baptized by one Spirit so as to form one body—whether Jews or Gentiles, slave or free—and we were all given the one Spirit to drink. Even so the body is not made up of one part but of many.

Now if the foot should say, "Because I am not a hand, I do not belong to the body," it would not for that reason stop being part of the body. And if the ear should say, "Because I am not an eye, I do not belong to the body," it would not for that reason stop being part of the body. If the whole body were an eye, where would the sense of hearing be? If the whole body were an ear, where would the sense of smell be? But in fact God has placed the parts in the body, every one of them, just as he wanted them to be. If they were all one part, where would the body be? As it is, there are many parts, but one body.

The eye cannot say to the hand, "I don't need you!" And the head cannot say to the feet, "I don't need you!" On the contrary, those parts of the body that seem to be weaker are indispensable, and the parts that we think are less honorable we treat with special honor. And the parts that are unpresentable are treated with special modesty, while our presentable parts need no special treatment. But God has put the body together, giving greater honor to the parts that lacked it, so that there should be no division in the body, but that its parts should have equal concern for each other. If one part suffers, every part suffers with it; if one part is honored, every part rejoices with it.

Now you are the body of Christ, and each one of you is a part of it. And God has placed in the church first of all apostles, second prophets, third teachers, then miracles, then gifts of healing, of helping, of guidance, and of different kinds of tongues. Are all apostles? Are all prophets? Are all teachers? Do all work miracles? Do all have gifts of healing? Do all speak in tongues? Do all interpret? Now eagerly desire the greater gifts.

1 Corinthians 12:4-31

Once again, Paul begins by emphasizing the variety of gifts, as well as the one God who grants them and in whose service they must be employed. Unity and diversity is again the theme. Once more, it is stressed that the gifts are distributed among followers of Jesus not as they determine, but as the Spirit determines.

This aspect—the Spirit determining who gets what gift—is crucial to understanding both spiritual gifts and the nature of the Body. It has been suggested that Jesus operated in all of the gifts during his earthly ministry, and possibly that Paul did so as well, with the implication that our goal should be to seek for and practice as many of the gifts as possible—potentially, all of them. With regard to Jesus, this claim is unhelpful, and with regard to Paul, it is demonstrably false. Jesus clearly had every ability necessary for accomplishing the specific mission that the Father had for him during his earthly ministry, but he also said to his disciples that, "Whoever believes in me will do the works I have been doing, and they will do even greater things than these, because I am going to the Father" (John 14:12), implying that the later church would exhibit different gifts, or gifts to a greater degree, than those he exhibited in his earthly ministry. Where the body and gifts are discussed in the epistles, they apply to how the Church is supposed to function as a unit, and how each individual contributes. Trying to describe Jesus' ministry using the category of spiritual gifts is anachronistic: Jesus can't be thought of simply as one member of his own body, so the language of giftedness that we see in the epistles really doesn't apply to him one way or the other.

With regard to Paul's ministry, it's quite clear that he did not, in fact, have all of the gifts, and it would be completely contrary to his point if he did. He makes clear in 1 Corinthians 3:5-10 the differences between his ministry and that of Apollos, who came after him and furthered the work that Paul had started. A study of Paul and Barnabas in the book of Acts clearly reveals the different gifts of each one: Barnabas was the consummate pastor with a heart of gold, sacrificially giving to God's work (Acts 4:36-37), sticking his neck out for Paul when everyone else was still afraid of him (Acts 9:26-27), taking charge of the fledgling church at Antioch, taking Paul under his wing to minister at that church, and bringing famine relief to the Judean believers (Acts 11:22-30). When opposition reared its head on a missionary journey, however, it is Paul who comes to the fore (Acts 13:6-12), and he is the dominant figure in the narrative from that point forward—up to this point Luke has referred to "Barnabas and Saul," while after this point he refers to "Paul and Barnabas."

This difference in gifts is probably the main issue that caused the split between Paul and Barnabas at the outset of the second missionary journey (Acts 15:39). Barnabas has a kind heart toward John Mark and wants to include him on a return visit to the churches that had been founded on their previous journey; Paul doesn't want to take John Mark because he had deserted them on their previous journey, and what we now call Paul's second missionary journey would blaze new territory into Macedonia and Greece (Acts 15:36-41; 16:1-18:22). The gifts are evident: Barnabas has pastoral concern for John Mark, while Paul has the missionary's passion to press into new territory and jettison whatever (or whomever) might jeopardize that mission. It's not a matter of who was right and who was wrong in the dispute; it's a matter of different members pursuing different gifts. Each one probably did exactly what God intended for him to do, even if the actual dispute described in Acts was not a godly way for the two to part.

At any rate, it's quite clear that Barnabas and Apollos had different gifts from the ones that Paul exhibited; and it's therefore impossible that Paul had all of them. Moreover, Paul makes clear that having all the gifts as an individual is not even desirable: that's not how the Body is intended to work. God wants us to be different: it enhances our unity, because *it forces us to have to rely on one another.* If God were to grant to any individual all the gifts necessary for the mission of Christ to be accomplished, there would be no point to having a group of people working together to accomplish it. With our tendency toward division and strife, a group of individuals in which each possessed everything necessary to accomplish the mission would find it impossible to work together. With the body working as it is intended to work, we have to depend on one another. We each contribute but no one gets the glory, because no one could have done it himself. All the glory goes to Christ.

All this makes sense of the central section of this chapter, verses 15-26. Paul deals with two separate situations: one in which a part of the body minimizes its own role and concludes that it is not, in fact, a part of the body at all; and another in which a part of the body does not recognize its need of another, and thus implicitly excludes other parts from the body. Both of these are errors, because they don't recognize the interdependence of the body as a whole.

The first error we might call gift denial: the problem is that those in question don't recognize their gifts to be necessary to the body. More than likely, they don't identify them as being gifts at all. They see no value to the contribution they've been enabled to make to the body, and may be paralyzed by their inability to do other things that they consider more valuable. "Now if the foot should say, 'Because I am not a hand, I do not belong to the body,' it would not for that reason stop being part of the body." The foot does not merely minimize its own function; it does so *because it is not a hand.* It is comparison with another gift, one that appears more necessary, that causes it to minimize its own contribution. This comparison might simply be due to a sense of inferiority in that person, but it also might arise from a church culture that does not value that member's gift, or more likely, exalts another gift to the point where that's the only gift that matters.

The second error is gift exaltation, where the people in question don't recognize their need of other people's gifts. We can easily see that it is merely the flip side of the first error: these are people whose gifts are recognized to be necessary to the body and who don't recognize the necessity of the gifts of others. "The eye cannot say to the hand, 'I don't need you!'" Apparently that was exactly what was being said, either overtly or by implication, by some to others in the Corinthian church. Oddly enough, this can also be done by denying that the gift being exalted is, in fact, a gift at all. If it is a gift, and if gifts are properly understood, then it will be recognized that not everyone will possess this gift, and so not everyone is responsible for using it. However, if it is not recognized as a gift, then it can be imposed as an obligation upon others, a phenomenon that C. Peter Wagner calls "gift projection." From this situation comes the feeling of inferiority among those who are trying and failing to operate in a gift that they've never been given, and their consequent minimizing of the contribution they could make if they were free to use the gifts they do have. The two phenomena, gift denial and gift exaltation, are complementary errors that nearly always occur in the same context.

Paul makes clear that these errors harm the body. Collectively, we suffer when certain members are not functioning and others are given too great a position. In fact, he makes it clear that apparent importance can be deceiving: "Those parts of the body that seem to be weaker are indispensable, and the parts that we think are less honorable we treat with special honor." Internal organs—those we rarely think about—are much more necessary to life than those whose functions we regard more highly. The sexual organs, which we cover, are quite important to our sense of identity. The larger context of 1 Corinthians 12-14 seems to suggest that the Corinthians had overly exalted the gift of tongues, beyond any actual usefulness or benefit to the body. It appears from Paul's comparison in chapter 14 that other gifts, particularly prophecy, had been neglected in the Corinthians' focus on tongues, and correcting this abuse was a primary reason for Paul's extensive discussion of gifts and the body in his letter to them. The heart of the issue was that the gifts were not being used in love—that is to say, they were not being used for the benefit of the body as a whole, but rather were being used by individuals to exalt their own status. It was a single symptom of an overall issue of division that plagued the Corinthian church. This kind of division is one cost of gift exaltation.

Paul's rhetorical questions at the end of the chapter—"Are all apostles? Are all prophets?"—reemphasize the fact that no one can have all the gifts, and that no single gift is possessed by every believer. This is all intentional on the part of the Holy Spirit, who "distributes them to each one, just as he determines." Paul is describing how the church is supposed to function, which is completely different from how people expect it to function. People expect it to be a singular effort to which everyone contributes the same sort of thing, while God has in mind a complex effort to which everyone contributes entirely different sorts of things, but all cooperate and move toward a singular goal.

The final passage Paul uses to describe spiritual gifts and the Body is in Ephesians:

> Make every effort to keep the unity of the Spirit through the bond of peace. There is one body and one Spirit, just as you were called to one hope when you were called; one Lord, one faith, one baptism; one God and Father of all, who is over all and through all and in all.
>
> But to each one of us grace has been given as Christ apportioned it. This is why it says:
> "When he ascended on high,
> he took many captives
> and gave gifts to his people."
> (What does "he ascended" mean except that he also descended to the lower, earthly regions? He who descended is the very one who ascended higher than all the heavens, in order to fill the whole universe.) So Christ himself gave the apostles, the prophets, the evangelists, the pastors and teachers, to equip his people for works of service, so that the body of Christ may be built up until we all reach unity in the faith and in the knowledge of the Son

of God and become mature, attaining to the whole measure of the fullness of Christ.

Ephesians 4:3-13

Once again, Paul begins by appealing to unity on the part of his readers, an important aspect of the entire book of Ephesians, which describes God as bringing together Jewish and Gentile believers into a unified people of God. The singularity of both the body and of the Spirit who gives the gifts is emphasized. But once again, diversity comes to the fore as gifts to the individual members of the one body are introduced: "To each one of us grace has been given as Christ apportioned it."

In this case, the gifts enumerated are apostles, prophets, evangelists, and pastors and teachers. Rather than being expressed through abstract nouns such as prophecy or evangelism, the gifts here are expressed as individuals: the persons who work in these gifts are actually considered to be gifts to the church themselves. This is a good perspective to add to the one provided by the other gift lists: the gifts are not merely attributes that we as individuals exercise. We ourselves are gifts to the body and are responsible to use our abilities and talents in the interest of the body.

This list of gifts is also sometimes referred to as the "fivefold ministry" gifts, the idea being that these are five titled positions that collectively describe the leadership of the church. There are problems with this view, not the least of which is that the Greek grammar suggests pretty strongly that "pastors and teachers" should be considered as one category rather than two. Moreover, other, more extensive discussions of actual offices in the church (mostly in the pastoral epistles) refer to "elders," "overseers," and "deacons," rather than to any of the categories mentioned here in Ephesians. It would seem more reasonable to view this list as being gifts than as official, titled offices of the church. What matters is not the names that are given to various offices, but rather whether we allow and encourage these divinely-granted abilities to be exercised for the benefit of the body.

Some churches, following the "fivefold" model, have commissioned prophets as titled and commissioned leaders. This is especially problematic, since we have Old Testament precedent indicating that, unlike priests or kings, prophets could come from any parentage or walk of life, and were generally outsiders to the established hierarchies of Israel. Rather than reinforcing the authorities that existed, the prophets' function was actually to challenge them, even though the priests and kings themselves had been established by God. So the idea of a church having official prophets seems a bit strained against the biblical evidence. However, otherwise unofficial laypeople, exercising a gift of prophecy and sometimes challenging human authorities in a church, would be thoroughly biblical.

In response to the idea that the "fivefold ministry" refers specifically to the official leadership of a church, Alan Hirsch counters that all believers fall somewhere within the "ministry matrix" of these five gifts, exhibiting one or more that reflect their individual passions, callings, and personality. He supports this understanding by citing "to each one of us grace has been given" from verse 7 and applying it to "Christ himself gave" in verse 11. The point is that Jesus gave these gifts to the whole church, not just to a specific class of leaders, and so each one of us embodies one or more of them. Hirsch's interpretation founders on the fact that if he takes apostles, prophets, evangelists, and pastors and teachers to include all of God's people, it would force him to take the subsequent phrase, "to equip his people for works of service," as, "to equip one another for continued use of the fivefold gifts." This is not at all a natural reading of the text, which seems rather to indicate that the individuals using these gifts are themselves regarded as a gift to the rest of the body, who are thereby equipped to serve in other ways.[11]

So the group of gifts discussed in Ephesians, although appearing a bit different from other gift lists, is essentially the same. There may be people who have a pastoral or teaching relationship to others who don't necessarily hold such an office, or people who evangelize effectively through the power of the Holy Spirit, who don't necessarily have that title. The purpose of these gifts, once again, is to do different things in order to accomplish a unified purpose, which as stated here is "to equip his people for works of service, so that the body of Christ may be built up." While some have argued that "works of service" is yet another gift, or the default gift for anyone not in the "fivefold" category (sometimes identified with

---

[11] Hirsch, Alan. *The Forgotten Ways: Reactivating The Missional Church.* Grand Rapids, MI: Brazos Press, 2006. 158, 257-58. Print.

"helping" in 1 Cor. 12:28), it may simply be a catch-all term for everyone else using whatever gifts they have been granted by God. The purpose of the fivefold gifts, then, would be to help develop others in their own gifts—that would be what "equipping" them would mean.

The point of this extended discussion of gifts is to illustrate how God clearly intends for the church to operate: a variety of different people working together in a variety of different ways in order to accomplish a single coordinated purpose, expressed in the Great Commission as making disciples. The reason that this is necessary is that making disciples as it is typically understood reduces down to evangelism—that is, overtly "sharing the gospel" with those who are unbelievers. Through gift exaltation and gift projection, evangelism is first denied as being a specific gift that some have and others don't, and then imposed upon everyone as an obligation. Anyone who is not proactively seeking out others with whom to share the gospel is considered unconcerned about the lost and avoiding their responsibility in Christ. If we understand how spiritual gifts are supposed to work and what making disciples really entails, we will understand that evangelism is one gift among many that is given to some believers and not to others, that exercising any gift plays a part in fulfilling the Great Commission even if it does not have a direct relationship to reaching the lost, and that developing people who already have made a commitment to Christ is as much a part of fulfilling the Commission as is reaching out to those who have made no such commitment yet.

Sometimes these implications are avoided by appealing to the concept of roles, as distinct from gifts. The idea of roles entails that even if we are each given specific gifts, there are a lot of things that all believers are required to do, including such things as giving, serving, and faith, which are also included among specific gift lists. Therefore, it would appear that spiritual gifts can be and often are simply enhanced abilities to do what all believers are called upon to do. When someone especially gifted to do something is not available, a particular situation may require that someone not especially gifted in that area nonetheless adopt the role of someone who is. We all need to be prepared to pray for healing for someone, even if we don't have a specific healing gift. We are all required to step out in faith in certain circumstances, even if we don't all have a gift of faith. Peter's command to "Always be prepared to give an answer to everyone who asks you to give the reason for the hope that you have" (1 Peter 3:15), applies to all his readers, even those not gifted in evangelism.

While this concept of roles is reasonable as far as it goes, in some cases it becomes the default answer to the concept of gifts. With a brief appeal to roles, the entire biblical theology of gifts gets waived aside. Focusing on gifts, in fact, is often viewed as a cop-out, an easy way to avoid doing what an individual believer doesn't want to do.

But this appeal to roles is entirely extra-biblical. The concept of roles, unlike that of gifts, is foreign to the text of scripture, although it might be inferred from various passages—Peter, for example, was considered an apostle to the Jews (Galatians 2:8) and yet was used on one significant occasion to evangelize the Gentile household of Cornelius (Acts 10). But there is nothing to suggest that anyone was ever expected to live out their lives performing a role for which they were not gifted; much less that all believers were to live out their lives performing one particular role for which only a few persons were gifted. If that were the case, it would undermine everything that the Bible has to say about gifts, about the body, about unity in diversity.

Looking at the theology of gifts as simply a cop-out to avoid the necessity of personal evangelism seriously misses the overall mission of making disciples. Making disciples is far more encompassing than simply getting people to make a decision for Jesus, or to repeat the words to a prayer. It takes a wide variety of gifts—and therefore a significant number of people—to bring unbelievers from a state of knowing nothing about God or being actively hostile to what they do know, to recognizing their responsibility to him and their need for forgiveness from him, to making a commitment, to following through and actually living that commitment out, to learning a whole new worldview and making the continuing changes that are necessary to grow into maturity as a believer. Every step along this path is crucial, and therefore every person's unique gifts that contribute to this process in any way, however indirectly, are important and needed. It might very well be that pulling people out of the areas in which they feel the most fulfilled and pushing them all into one small portion of the spectrum hinders not only the development of the entire process but also even the specific point that we are trying to focus on. God's ways are wiser than ours. If various gifts, various parts to play, various points along the spectrum is the plan he gave us, then maybe it works better than anything we could come up with in our own understanding.

What Is Discipleship, Anyway?

Much of this book has been an extended defense of the importance of discipleship relative to evangelism, which naturally brings up a question: What is discipleship, anyway? Discipleship is one of those words that gets treated as self-evident when it's really not. We use the word because it fits in well with the Great Commission's command to "make disciples," but that doesn't mean that we truly understand how to go about doing it. As a matter of fact, that may be one of the reasons why we focus on outreach and evangelism rather than discipleship: they're just easier to get our heads around. Most of us carry many unconscious assumptions about discipleship, assumptions that reveal what we consider to be important in living the Christian life.

Probably the most common assumption about discipleship is that it is essentially a learning process: learning the Bible and learning correct doctrine. A typical mode of discipling new believers is to put them into a class that teaches whatever doctrinal truths our fellowship regards as foundational, proof-texted with the biblical passages that form our canon-within-the-canon. From there, depending on the type of church, there may be more classes, Sunday

School or midweek, that provide an ever-broadening educational foundation for Christian life. This we may call intellectual discipleship.

Depending on one's faith tradition, intellectual discipleship may be the primary measure of spiritual growth. Some traditions become extremely detailed and elaborate, and establishing and defending correct doctrine are regarded as the primary goal of discipleship. Various sorts of catechisms or other teaching methods may be used, in some cases being required for confirmation in the faith. The primary focus would be that if faith involves believing in something, then the content of what one believes is extremely important. Truth is something to be defended. The proper response to unbelief or misplaced belief is rational argumentation. This type of faith tradition tends to produce people who are very articulate and passionate about their own church's theological positions. The ultimate goal of such a faith tradition generally culminates in a seminary education and professional ministry, which largely consists of passing along these positions and their intellectual underpinnings to a new generation. This subset of intellectual discipleship we may call doctrinal discipleship.

Other churches will have a different focus. In some, spiritual experiences are the primary mode of discipleship. Although there will be teaching going on in this type of church as well, there is an adamant distinction between what is considered cold, intellectualized "head knowledge" and a more deeply felt and experienced "heart knowledge." Once again, this takes different forms.

In some, it is the experience of worship that is sought, either in a high, formal, rich vein, or in the more popular, informal, passionate form found in Pentecostal traditions and increasingly in the wider evangelical community. Some will focus on such practices as fasting, meditation, or silence to enhance spiritual growth. Prayer is usually a significant emphasis in this type of tradition. The basic unifying idea behind all these separate threads is that the Christian life is to be experienced, not merely understood intellectually. Believers from this tradition will be encouraged continually to renew their first love, to immerse themselves in experiences that will raise them to a higher emotional and spiritual state. A person's spiritual life in this type of church will not be evaluated primarily by their doctrinal knowledge, but by their participation in worship services, spiritual retreats, or other experience-based events and personal practices. This may be called experiential discipleship.

Then there are traditions that focus on the interconnectedness of the body of Christ. Fellowship is the key focus here. All kinds of gatherings, from potlucks and picnics to various types of social events, are the lifeblood of these churches—or, as they are likely to call themselves, fellowships. Individual celebrations such as birthdays and anniversaries will be celebrated communally by the entire group; individual hardships will be borne by the group as a whole. You can count on people from this type of tradition to bring meals to people who are sick or recently bereaved. While other traditions may view this type of church body as nothing but a social club, it will view itself as taking seriously and acting upon the command to "Rejoice with those who rejoice; mourn with those who mourn" (Rom. 12:15). Jesus' parable of the Sheep and the Goats would have special relevance to these believers: "whatever you did for one of the least of these brothers and sisters of mine, you did for me" (Matthew 25:40). Although the term "discipleship" may not often be used in this context, the socialization process that one experiences in this environment has the effect of discipling in interpersonal relationships. One's spiritual progress in this group is likely to be reflected in participation in events that bind the body together. This may be called relational discipleship.

A subgroup of relational discipleship is found in small-group ministries. Small groups are used in a variety of contexts and can foster any form of discipleship: they may be oriented toward teaching, or experience, or fellowship, and often their function is to provide the interpersonal experience of a small church within the structure of a larger church. They counter the depersonalized nature that a large church can have when an individual feels lost in a crowd. In some cases, small groups become support groups for people struggling with similar emotional issues, or similar forms of temptation. The intimacy of these groups can become intense. Other groups are self-consciously modeled on the example of Jesus and the twelve, the idea being that we need to recapture discipleship as Jesus did it, focusing on the holistic teaching, shared experience, and guided mission that Jesus conducted with his disciples. These types of groups would be heightened forms of relational discipleship, but would also incorporate aspects of other forms of discipleship.

In still other traditions, discipleship will be reflected in service. Rejecting intellectualism, emotionalism, and simply cultivating relationships, this form of discipleship would channel believers into serving in soup kitchens, building homes with such groups as Habitat for Humanity, and finding various ways of helping anyone in need. By contrast with traditions centered on fellowship, this service-oriented model would generally be focused on those outside the body of believers, and is almost always regarded as at least partially a form of outreach. One's spiritual progress here tends to be evaluated on the basis of how much one is involved in service to others. Lack of participation, especially in group efforts, is generally seen as self-centeredness and a form of spiritual immaturity. This we may term service-oriented discipleship.

Finally, discipleship can be oriented toward evangelism and outreach. Service-oriented discipleship tends to be a subgroup of this type, although in some cases it merely overlaps and service is regarded as an end unto itself. Most self-conscious forms of discipleship will regard the mature disciple being able to "reproduce" as the end goal. But in some cases, the process of discipleship largely involves memorizing the Romans Road to Salvation, the Four Spiritual Laws, Evangelism Explosion, key principles from the Purpose-Driven Life, or other evangelistic strategies, along with ways to find opportunities to share one's faith. In other cases, the focus is on such means of outreach as passing out bottled water at public events or the famous confession booth in *Blue Like Jazz.* Regardless of strategy, the point of this type of discipleship is to help believers learn how to do evangelism or pre-evangelism. Other types of discipleship are viewed as mere distractions from our real purpose of leading others to Christ. People in this type of church will tend to be evaluated by their individual evangelistic outreach endeavors, and even more on their participation in such outreach endeavors that are created and promoted by the church body as a whole.

So what type of discipleship is the right one? This question can be divided into two separate questions. The first is, What is the desired result of the discipleship process—that is, what does a mature, fully-discipled person look like? The second is, What process is most likely to produce that sort of person? And as much as possible, we should derive the answer from Scripture, rather than simply trying to intuit or rationalize the answer.

The Greek word *teleos,* often translated as "mature," signifies completion, something which has achieved its expected and desired goal. It is also often translated as "perfect," but the central idea isn't flawlessness, but rather full development. The first place that this Greek word appears in the New Testament is in Jesus' statement, "Be perfect *(teleioi),* therefore, as your heavenly Father is perfect" (Matt. 5:48). The statement is in the form of a command; it is also the ultimate desired goal of any believer. How can one hope for anything better than perfection? Since it combines both of these concepts, tracing how *teleos* is used in the New Testament should help us understand what the goal of the discipleship process should be.[12]

The passage just referred to caps off the "antitheses" section of the Sermon on the Mount, in which Jesus contrasts six examples of the ethic of the Kingdom with the Mosaic Law (or first-century misinterpretations of the Law). His statement to be "perfect" (or mature) should then reflect a strict renunciation of lust and anger (not just the outward manifestations of adultery and murder), divorce, oaths, retribution, and hatred of enemies. In the antithesis that forms the immediate context of his command to be perfect, Jesus tells us that we should actively love and pray for our enemies, the ones who persecute us. He makes clear that by refusing to do so, we fail to distinguish ourselves from obvious sinners and those who simply do not know God. One object of discipleship, then, would involve instilling a heightened desire to live out the spirit of the Law, and not simply the explicit text, including self-sacrificial love toward all, and especially toward those who would persecute us (Matt. 5, esp. vv. 43-48).

In another passage Jesus tells the rich young ruler, "If you want to be perfect *(telaios)*, go, sell your possessions and give to the poor, and you will have treasure in heaven. Then come, follow me" (Matt. 19:21). There are various interpretations regarding what Jesus' response meant—whether he was challenging the man's claim to have loved

---

[12] *Teleos* in the New Testament: Mat. 5:48; 19:21; Rom. 12:2; 1Co. 2:6; 13:10; 14:20; Eph. 4:13; Php. 3:15; Col. 1:28; 4:12; Heb. 5:14; 9:11; Jas. 1:4,17,25; 3:2; 1Jn. 4:18.

his neighbor as himself since he had been young (vv. 19-20), was offering an additional command for a higher-tier category of disciple, was presenting a deal-breaker in order to force the man to stop thinking in terms of self-righteousness, or was pointing out a specific hurdle to that particular man because of his own sinful attachment to wealth. Regardless of which particular understanding we have of Jesus' statement, he clearly illustrates that clinging to affluence is a barrier to full discipleship. So another objective of discipleship would be overcoming an earthly attachment to physical possessions and replacing it with devotion to following Jesus.

In Ephesians 4:13, Paul equates maturity with attaining unity with one another, attaining knowledge of Jesus, becoming like Jesus, and not being overly influenced ("tossed to and fro") by doctrinal fads and cunning human schemes. It is a product of the gifts designated in verse 11, and is characterized by "speaking the truth in love" (vv. 11-15).

In 1 Corinthians 14:20, Paul appeals to his readers to "stop thinking like children. In regard to evil be infants, but in your thinking be adults" (*teleioi*, "mature" ESV, NASB). This comes near the culmination of his discussion on spiritual gifts, in which the overall point is that spiritual gifts must be used in love and for the benefit of the body, not for the selfish aggrandizement of the person demonstrating the gift. In the immediate context, the sense appears to be that focusing on tongues for the sake of tongues is spiritually childish; recognizing the need for others to be instructed is a sign of maturity (vv. 18-22).

Paul's prison epistles give more perspective on maturity. He writes to the believers in Philippi that the mature have the attitude he has just described regarding himself, which involves letting go of any human (or law-keeping) attainment of righteousness, trusting in Jesus for His righteousness, leaving the past behind, and striving forward for the prize, which he has already identified as resurrection from the dead. What seems key in this passage is that sharing in Jesus' sufferings and becoming like him in his death has in some sense replaced the need to live up to Torah righteousness; so emulating Jesus seems to be the "striving" that Paul is talking about (Phil. 3:12-15). Similarly, to the Colossians he writes, "He is the one we proclaim, admonishing and teaching everyone with all wisdom, so that we may present everyone fully mature in Christ" (Col. 1:28). Maturity in the immediate context is a result of Paul warning and teaching people. But this comes in the context of Paul's own suffering for the gospel, a suffering that in some sense completes Jesus' own afflictions (Col. 1:24). Since Paul is an example of the mature believer he is attempting to produce, this maturity should be exhibited by a willingness to suffer in this present life for the sake of the gospel (cf. Acts 14:22).

In Hebrews 5:14, the author distinguishes between those who need doctrinal "milk" and the mature, who are ready for "solid food," characterized by their practiced discernment between good and evil. The subsequent passage goes on to begin warnings against apostasy and to encourage perseverance in the faith, which necessitates perseverance in what is right, recognizing Jesus as being a better priest of a better covenant with a better sacrifice and better promises than those of the old covenant. There is, however, a heightened sense of the necessity of obedience: "For if we go on sinning deliberately after receiving the knowledge of the truth, there no longer remains a sacrifice for sins, but a fearful expectation of judgment, and a fury of fire that will consume the adversaries" (10:26-27).

This catalogue of the contexts of the word *teleos* pretty clearly indicates that maturity is not a simple, monolithic idea in the New Testament. To sum up, spiritual maturity appears to involve several factors: reaching out in active love to enemies, rather than indulging the impulse toward retaliation (Matt. 5:48); preferring following Jesus to material wealth or comfort (Matt. 19:21); being transformed by our minds being renewed (Rom. 12:2); understanding spiritual truths spiritually, rather than through natural rationalism (1 Cor. 12:6); using spiritual gifts in order to benefit the body as a whole, rather than to draw attention and praise to the individual exercising the gift (1 Cor. 14:20); having one's focus be on Jesus' righteousness and being willing to suffer for the sake of "the prize" (Phil. 3:15, Col. 1:28); having an assurance of God's will (Col. 4:12); having a practiced discernment between good and evil, recognizing that Jesus' infinitely good sacrifice for us must be responded to by our obedience (Heb. 5:14); perseverance through trials and testing of our faith (Jas. 1:4); controlling one's tongue and thereby, oneself overall (Jas. 3:2); and having the kind of love for both God and others that eclipses any fear of judgment (1 Jn. 4:18).

So what kind of discipleship process will produce this kind of multifaceted result? Simple biblical instruction won't do it: we all know the type of person who uses biblical knowledge to argue viciously over doctrine in internet chat rooms. That is clearly not the goal. Neither will spiritual experience: there are those who are constantly hunting down the next spiritual buzz, but exhibit little of the fruit of the Spirit. Relational discipleship by itself can produce insular cliques. Trying to reproduce the experience of Jesus and the twelve tends to founder on the cultural differences between the first-century Middle East and modern life. A service orientation by itself, without a biblical foundation and spiritual experience, becomes indistinguishable from secular charitable work. Evangelism, without the counterbalance of any of the other focal points, can simply produce the sort of annoying person who shares their faith in a manner unlikely to win anyone over, or if it does, takes people through a revolving door, because there's nothing on the inside other than strategies for bringing more people in. None of these results looks much like the complex biblical picture of maturity.

It begins to be obvious that a variety of discipleship avenues must work together concurrently to begin to approach the goal of maturity as described in scripture. One needs to know the Bible, obviously, in order to begin to put it into practice. One needs fellowship and the support of others, to achieve the kind of unity and sense that the body of Christ is larger than oneself which several passages relating to maturity describe. One needs the direct impact of spiritual experience—it's reasonably clear that a supernatural work has to accomplish the goal of discipleship. It's not merely the effect of human effort, study, or relationship. One needs to be involved in service to others; one needs to have a heart for those who are lost and for the continued growth of everyone. In fact, all the modes of discipleship mentioned earlier have their place.

And so, the process of discipleship must necessarily be larger than what is generally imagined. In some sense, everything we do as the body of Christ is a part of discipleship. This does not mean, however, that because we can lump everything under the discipleship heading, we can therefore rest easy and assume that discipleship is taking place as it should. The danger is that each one of us has a greater affinity for some of these aspects than others. Leaders, in particular, have a tendency toward wanting to steer people toward the type of ministry that the leader has the most passion for and is most gifted in. Evangelistic leaders will tend to want everyone to become an evangelist; scholarly leaders want everyone to become a scholar; relational leaders just want us all to get along.

In this lies the great obstacle, but also the key, to effective discipleship. The obstacle is our innate tendency to press people into our own molds, and people in congregations feel that pressure. It's great for those whose gifts are a close match to those of the leader, but for those who have different gifts, their choices are often either to conform or to move on. It frustrates them and heaps guilt on them where the Holy Spirit never intended. Is it any wonder that it is just at this point, where people have absorbed a basic level of biblical knowledge, spiritual experience, and fellowship among believers, that they seem to stall? Church leaders, trying to make everyone become like themselves, bemoan the fact that spiritual development peters out just beyond infancy, and can't understand why this is the case.

The key to effective discipleship, on the other hand, lies is in recognizing that just as maturity is complex and multifaceted, so is the process of discipleship, as is the end result. If we understand that congregations are composed of people with different gifts—that they necessarily and by God's design have different gifts—then we need to recognize that a cookie-cutter approach to discipleship is exactly the wrong way to go about it. Discipleship simply doesn't look the same for everybody.

Many churches and faith traditions understand that people have different gifts, and most pastors know that there are people they need to rely on who have different gifts than they themselves do. But when we divorce giftedness from discipleship, we create a disjunction that God never intended. We essentially tell people, "It's great that you can cook, and you're invaluable in fostering fellowship, but we're never going to accept you as a fully-discipled believer until you've completed our year-long theological training course." "It's nice that you have such a great grasp of scripture, but until you become more outgoing and start witnessing to people on the street, you're really not moving beyond intellectualism." "We really appreciate your service-oriented heart, but if you're not attending every revival meeting, you're just missing out on what God has for you." We fail to recognize that maturity means growing into ourselves, into our identities as unique individuals called by God to play our own part as no one else can.

All the babies in a hospital nursery are really very similar. They're not very different in size, not very different in ability. They all cry, they all need to be fed and changed and held. The various heights that they will all grow to, the diverse languages they will speak, the distinctions in physical and athletic abilities they will have, the dissimilar intellectual bents they will display, the different personalities they will exhibit—all these things are very nearly invisible while children are still babies. They don't come to the fore until years later. In the same way, the requirements of people who have just been reborn spiritually are similar—they all need to begin understanding the Bible, they all need to begin relationships with other believers, they all need to work through healing from the brokenness of life without God. This deceives us into thinking that discipleship is all one thing for everyone: everyone starts out needing pretty much the same thing.

But babies grow into children, who grow into adolescents and then into adults. As they grow, they have different aptitudes and different needs. One excels in sports, another in academics, another has an artistic bent, and still another is mechanically inclined. One is overly impulsive, another too cautious. Any parent with more than one child understands that it is impossible to deal with them all in exactly the same way, and unwise to try. One child needs very firm discipline while another melts under a stern word. Perceptive parents make room for all of these differences, and encourage their children in whatever area each child gravitates toward.

Similarly, as believers begin to develop, what they're naturally good at and passionate about is going to begin to show. It's at that stage that the discipleship process needs to recognize the differences among people. While striving to achieve a base level of balance—no one should merely be relational, without even a rudimentary understanding of the Bible, and vice versa—we should encourage people to develop in the gifts that they have, *and recognize that development to be discipleship.* A mature missionary isn't going to look like a mature giver, who isn't going to look like a mature teacher, who isn't going to look like a mature administrator or prophet or evangelist. We need to stop expecting them to.

So as it turns out, discipleship is not the process by which I, as a leader, get everyone to become as much like me as possible. It's a process by which I, as a leader, facilitate the development of every follower of Jesus whom God has entrusted to my care to become *themselves* at the highest level, to the highest degree. It's using every tool possible: services, classrooms, home fellowships, personal relationships, service projects, evangelism opportunities, and any other means we can think of, to help them develop into unique people using their distinct gifts and talents for the benefit of the body and to participate in the restoration of the world which God began at the

Resurrection and will complete upon his return. That's what maturity looks like. That's what effective discipleship is supposed to be.

The Analogy of Growth

Discussing discipleship and giftedness leads us back to discussing the body. We sometimes forget that "the body" is an analogy—a visual image that the Apostle Paul used to describe the unity and diversity of God's people. The analogy of the body, in many people's minds, then leads to an analogy of growth. The logic goes this way: the church is not an organization, but an organism. Healthy organisms grow. If the church is healthy, it will grow. A lack of growth indicates a lack of health.

Like many seemingly simple and obvious analogies, this one fails to pass scrutiny.

The first thing to note is that the biblical use of "the body" is being misappropriated. One of the problems that most believers have in interpreting Scripture is handling metaphors and analogies. If Jesus says, "You are the salt of the earth" and "You are the light of the world," we tend to take these statements as all-encompassing facts, and then tease out what different types of properties exist in salt and light for which we may find some spiritual application. We ignore the context of Jesus' statements and the fact that these are mutually illuminating metaphors. Jesus was pointing out that salt and light make themselves evident by their effects on other things, and that in the same way, followers of Jesus should live in such a way that they have an effect on those around them. His point had nothing to do with any other properties of salt and light to which we may imaginatively attach some other spiritual application.

Most of us repeat the same mistake when we look at other metaphors and analogies that are used in Scripture. When we come to the term, "body," we tend not to recognize that it, too, is a metaphor, a way of speaking that helps us to view God's people in a particular light. As described in the chapter on spiritual gifts, the analogy of the body is used only by Paul among the New Testament writers, and it's always used with regard to spiritual gifts, specifically to illustrate the point of unity and diversity among God's people. We are not only allowed to be different, we are created to be different, we are supposed to be different, by God's design, in order to cooperate in accomplishing God's overall purpose. That is how the analogy of the body is used in scripture; that is what it means.

So when we take "body" to mean "organism," and then take a single attribute of organisms—growth—to be the most significant aspect, and then make that aspect into a mandate for the church, so that "the church is like a body" becomes "it is your responsibility to make the church grow," we're stretching the biblical evidence just a little bit. The fact that the Bible uses the term "body" to refer to the people of God does not inherently mean that every attribute of a physical body applies to the people of

God. The inference that body equals organism equals growth doesn't even work all that well. Physical organisms generally do not grow indefinitely; their growth stops when they reach maturity. Continued growth past the point of maturity generally signifies such unhealthy conditions as obesity or cancer. It's possible that, at least on the local church level, unrestrained growth may indicate similarly negative conditions. Not all megachurches are filled with spiritually healthy people.[13]

All of this is not, of course, to suggest that people being added to the kingdom is a bad thing. It's just to argue that growth is not the best way to express this, unless it's very clear that what we mean is growth in numbers of a group, and not growth in size of an individual organism. The term "growth" is so pervasive in our thought that I use it throughout this very book, although I don't think it's really the best way to express the concept. It's interesting that in Acts, it is the "word of God"—not the church itself—that is said to "increase" (the same Greek word is also used to mean "grow"). That expression is then followed by the statement that "the number of the disciples multiplied greatly" (Acts 6:7). Subsequently, Luke uses phrases like "the word of God continued to flourish and grow" (Acts 20:24; sim. 19:20) with a probable similar multiplication of disciples envisioned. But it is the word of God that is said to grow, not the body or the church itself.

---

[13] I would like to gratefully acknowledge the contribution of Rich Tatum to many of the ideas in this chapter, especially in "What Willow Creek's 'Reveal' study really tells us...." *Blog Rodent*. N.p., 05 June 2008. Web. 18 Aug. 2012. <http://tatumweb.com/blog/2008/06/05/reveal/>.

When Luke wants to say what we mean when we say the church grew, he tells us that many people were "added to their number" (Acts 2:41, 47; 5:14).

The real problem lies not simply in a desire for more people to find and know God through the power of the gospel. One would hope that everyone who knows Jesus would want that. The real problem lies in an unhealthy focus on growth, especially in the local church, where issues of comparison, envy, self-elevation, and self-denigration plague ministry. Church leaders gauge the health and effectiveness of their ministries by whether the church is, or appears to be, growing or not. In cases where it is not, they frequently make radical changes or turn up the pressure on their congregations to try to force growth to happen. C. S. Lewis complained about this tendency in *Letters to Malcolm:*

> It looks as if [Anglican clergy] believed people can be lured to go to church by incessant brightenings, lightenings, lengthenings, abridgements, simplifications, and complications of the service.[14]

Lewis's issue, it seems clear, is not the specific merits or demerits of any of these possible changes in and of themselves. He is rather protesting against making changes for the specific purpose of "luring" people to church. Aside from being distracting to those who already attend and who are trying to worship God through the medium

---

[14] Lewis, C. S. *Letters to Malcolm: Chiefly on Prayer.* San Diego: Harcourt Brace Jovanovich, 1964. 4. Print.

of the service, it telegraphs the message that there is nothing really very important about what we do when we gather together. The only important thing is how many people we can draw.

If the analogy of growth were actually correct, and if continual growth really were a primary indicator of spiritual health, then focusing on methods to produce growth would still be the wrong way to go about the problem of restoring the body to health. If growth is an indicator, then it is merely a symptom, and treating a symptom does nothing at all to deal with the causes of that symptom. Guilting or haranguing or bribing people into outreach doesn't deal with the inner issues that make them reluctant to reach out in the first place. Bringing people in by hosting a concert, movie, show of athleticism, picnic, fair, or some other form of entertainment, and then pulling the bait-and-switch and giving a salvation message, isn't a very solid introduction to a Jesus who is open, honest, straightforward, and truthful. The same critique applies to teaching on relational evangelism if it involves strategies to form "intentional" relationships with the ulterior motive of leading someone to Christ. The problem doesn't lie in wanting to see people saved or in forming relationships with people who do not know Jesus yet. The problem lies in the idea of forming a relationship with a hidden agenda, one that cannot be what it appears to be on the surface.

The trouble with all of these evangelism strategies and growth tactics is staring us right in the face: if growth is an indicator of health, then all of these things should be completely unnecessary. To use the analogy for the sake of argument, an organism doesn't grow because it tries to grow. It simply grows as a result of the natural processes that occur as a result of health. So if we're concerned about the health of the church, then dealing with that should be the primary priority, and growth (according to the analogy) should take care of itself.

But let's forget about the analogy. Why are individual Christians often reluctant to share their faith with others? Some of the answers to this question have been dealt with in the chapters regarding spiritual gifts and models of outreach. But the primary reason why people are reluctant to share their faith is simply that they feel stalled in their own spiritual development. No one wants to reproduce what doesn't seem to be working in his own life. And to the extent that church leaders focus on the latest outreach strategy, they are neglecting the spiritual growth and development of the people who have been entrusted to their care. Jesus didn't tell Peter, "Get my sheep to reproduce." He told him to "Feed my sheep." Apparently the principle was that if the shepherd provides the feeding, the reproduction will take care of itself.

Which leads to another misused metaphor: that of reproduction. This is generally applied on a more individual level. Healthy organisms may not grow indefinitely, but they do tend to reproduce. And that is what the follower of Jesus is called to do: to reproduce new followers of Jesus. Lack of reproduction, in this view, is a failure to be what Jesus called us to be and do what he called us to do. Strategies for growth, as they have been termed above, are really strategies for reproduction. What could be wrong with that?

Well, what's wrong with that is that the analogy, although better, is still flawed. For one thing, biological reproduction involves the creating of a new organism that hadn't existed before; spiritual reproduction involves bringing people who are currently in existence into a new relationship with Jesus that they hadn't had previously. No one has to persuade a baby to be conceived; one does have to be persuaded to submit to the lordship of Christ. For another, the analogy still puts symptoms ahead of causes. If healthy organisms reproduce, and reproduction isn't happening, then we still need to deal with the health of the organism, not reproductive techniques.

If we're going to use this analogy of reproduction, the problem remains: how do we get people to spiritually reproduce? Some think the issue is one of motivation, so a combination of carrots and sticks, rewards and guilt, are used to try to motivate people. Some think the difficulty is one of technique, of simply not knowing how to go about the process, so various strategies are taught to believers in order to help them find ways of introducing the subject and winning people. But once again, the real trouble is very frequently that people don't feel as though they have something worthwhile to share with others. And therefore, all the encouragement and strategizing to support spiritual reproduction ends up being pointless.

Although flawed, the analogy of reproduction is actually instructive, because it points out a possible solution to the dilemma. Viewed strictly in biological terms, the main purpose of any organism would be to reproduce. That's the only way a species can endure. But human beings are virtually unique in the animal kingdom in that a great deal of growth and development need to take place before the person is physically, emotionally, socially, and morally equipped to have children and to take care of those children until they are able to become independent. Human beings require much more care and nurturing to reach healthy adulthood than practically any other animal. More to the point, human beings require a lot of care and nurturing that are not directly related to reproduction itself, but are nonetheless necessary for the person to get to the point of being able to reproduce.

If one applies this thought to spiritual reproduction, some insights present themselves. Once again, it is certainly not a precise analogy. Very often, people who are new believers are much more adept and enthusiastic at sharing their faith with others than those who have been believers for most of their lives. But spiritual growth and development do involve many things that are not immediately relevant to spiritual reproduction, yet are nonetheless necessary for spiritual health and maturity. When a mother is feeding her baby, she isn't consciously thinking about preparing her child to make her a grandmother someday. When a father plays catch with his sons, he's not thinking about making them socially ready for reproduction. Parents don't clothe and house their children, keep an eye on their homework and enforce curfews, give them chores and teach them responsibility, purely in order to get them ready for reproduction. But all of these things and more contribute in ways both straightforward and circuitous to the child being prepared for adulthood, for marriage, and for parenthood.

All of this nurturing and training is necessary to prepare children for their biological role of reproduction, among other things. Much of it is not, in the strictest sense, biologically necessary—although a healthy, well-adjusted person might be more likely to reproduce than a sickly or socially maladjusted person. But that's not the real point. Human beings have always viewed parenthood as more encompassing than simple biological reproduction, and that insight certainly applies to the Christian faith. There is a great deal of physical, intellectual, psychological, educational, and moral preparation that goes into preparing a child to be a parent. Most of that happens without any conscious intent for parenthood to be the ultimate goal. This should also be the case when discussing spiritual development: most of it doesn't need to have any explicit relationship to spiritual parenting, but it will have an effect on how effective the spiritual child will become in the process of drawing other people and discipling them.

Intentionality has become something of a buzzword in recent years: it is thought that if we can become aware of what our goals are, and intentionally focus on methods designed to achieve those goals, we may accomplish them more often and more successfully. Intentional evangelism and intentional discipleship are thought to be the means by which we can—and must—bring the church back from its lethargic lack of growth, mission, and purpose. In many ways, this is unobjectionable: sometimes one can get things done better by focusing more clearly on the goal.

But not all the time. And that's the trouble. If you tried to raise a child in an intentional fashion so that everything was purposely designed to prepare that child for reproduction and parenthood, you wouldn't necessarily get someone who had children sooner or had more children than someone else. You just might get someone on a psychiatrist's couch, trying to figure out how to overcome their relationship anxieties, or wondering why they scare off every potential suitor, or feel no sense of worth other than being a baby-making machine. If we started with the goal of reproduction and raised our children with that goal alone, there's a lot of responsible parenting that we wouldn't think to include, and a lot of things we might wrongly include. On the other hand, if we raise a child with our primary concern being the healthy development of that child, making sure they're nurtured and cared for, there's a decent shot that they will make us grandparents some day.

All this may seem to be pushing an analogy far beyond warrant, and perhaps it is. But attacking the perceived problem of a lack of growth or reproduction in the church head on, making intentional decisions that are supposed to solve the problem by stimulating growth through some program or strategy or motivational tool, can be the worst thing the leadership of a church can do. That's what thousands of frustrated pastors have done for a long time, and the results have been nothing short of disastrous. An awful lot of people in an awful lot of churches feel unloved, un-nurtured, undeveloped, unimportant. They've been told, both subtly and not, that their only value lies in being convert-making machines, and since they're not that good at making converts, or since they don't see the point in converting someone to the same level of frustrated spirituality that they have themselves, they give up. Not having the nerve to quit the team, they sit on the sidelines and endure the scorn of the coach, who just can't see why they're reluctant to get in the game.

The analogy of growth is simply counterproductive, especially when it becomes—as it usually does—the controlling concept of how we view the church. It's transparently clear that Jesus did not place growth as a central priority in his own ministry. After feeding the five thousand, he left for the opposite side of the Sea of Galilee, and when the crowds found him there, he alienated them by challenging them on their motivations. So many people left him that Jesus asked the twelve if they were going to leave as well (John 6:66-67). Jesus focused not on the numerical growth of the movement he was starting but on the spiritual development of those who were following him, and especially on those whom he had chosen. We would be wise to imitate him in that.

Why the Persecuted Church Grows

While focusing on numerical growth for its own sake can be counterproductive, it can still be interesting and instructive to observe where growth has happened, especially under conditions in which one might think it would be unlikely. In his book *The Forgotten Ways,* Alan Hirsch asks a very interesting question: why is it that the early church, under persecution, had such remarkable growth? Similarly, why did the 20th century Chinese church, under persecution by the Communist regime, experience similar exponential growth? What is it about churches that have social hostility rather than support, little if any institutional foundation, lack of professional leadership, few buildings or "sacred spaces," and other seeming disadvantages as compared with the contemporary Western church—why do they grow at an amazing rate while the contemporary Western church seems to be in irreversible decline?

Hirsch's answer is that the very advantages that were conferred to the church in "Christendom" (the post-Constantinian church that took hold throughout Europe and the Americas) are the things that have combined to hold it back. Having buildings and a professional clergy create the need for generating constant income, so the church loses its focus on going into the world and being salt and light, by having to concern itself with sustaining its ever-increasing material needs. Becoming institutional in nature creates a milieu of power politics which corrupts the basic message that Jesus is Lord over all. More recently, our participation in a consumer culture creates a situation in which local churches try to attract people through programs and entertaining services in comfortable buildings with lots of convenient parking—which, of course, escalates the need for a continued influx of money. The attractional nature of the modern church—focusing on drawing people to services and events—subverts the command of Jesus to be salt and light in the world. This focus of attention being given to attracting more people has led to a church in a state of perpetual stagnation.

All this raises a question: obviously it's not simply the *absence* of institutions, professional clergy, buildings, and the like that caused the tremendous growth of the early church. There must have been something else, something that got eclipsed or crowded out, something that flourished before the institutionalization of the church became a reality, something that seems to come to life again in situations where the church finds itself driven underground by persecution, as happened in China during Mao's Cultural Revolution. Hirsch calls this factor "Missional DNA," or mDNA for short. Just as biological DNA is self-replicating and is responsible for many different aspects of an organism as it grows, mDNA self-replicates and guides the growth and development of the church. Hirsch describes six central components of mDNA, or "apostolic genius," to which he attributes the growth of the church in non-institutional situations: Jesus is Lord, disciple-making, missional-incarnational impulse, apostolic environment, organic systems, and what Hirsch calls *communitas*.

The best place to see these concepts fleshed out is in *The Forgotten Ways* itself. I don't propose to explain each one of these six principles individually, but I do have some impressions about the model as a whole. First of all, the principles of apostolic genius are basically Hirsch's creation—i.e., there's nothing in scripture that tells us in so many words that there are six principles to the expansion of a Jesus movement, and this is what they are. Hirsch has come up with this pattern by reflection on the Bible and Church history, which is a fine approach, but it's important that we don't give it the weight of revealed scriptural truth. Hirsch was looking for the solution to church growth and vitality—this autobiographical aspect of his leadership of South Melbourne Church of Christ (later South Melbourne Restoration Community) forms a significant part of *The Forgotten Ways*—and mDNA was what he came up with. As is true in many studies of this type, one often finds something similar to what one is looking for. So, for example, most of the elements of mDNA are consciously other-directed. *Communitas* is clearly contrasted with community on the basis that it is directed outward rather than inward. It's at least worth considering whether Hirsch found clear evidence of an outward focus in Christian communities in the New Testament record and in the documents we have from the first centuries of the church—and I mean an outward focus throughout the communities as a whole, and not merely in certain members—or whether Hirsch himself is outwardly-directed and therefore noted aspects of what he terms *communitas*. As discussed in an earlier chapter, the weight of the evidence in Acts suggests that the early Christian believers evidenced love for one another by self-sacrificial giving, and that outsiders took note of that.

Hirsch's concept of apostolic genius seems to work well as a useful model, rather than as actual fact. There are many aspects that may be true and biblical, but the overall impression that I received in reading the book was one of complexity. Each point of Hirsch's mDNA has a lot of subordinate aspects that Hirsh is asking us to keep in mind as we go about building missional communities. There is a significant amount of tension between this complexity on one hand and Hirsch's contention on the other that mDNA simply takes over and happens naturally when conditions prevail that prevent the institutional church from gaining the upper hand. That tension does not mean that Hirsch is wrong, necessarily—after all, the model he's using is biological DNA, the functions of which are incredibly complex. If God created the biological world to operate that way, it is certainly possible that he has created the spiritual world to work that way as well. Nonetheless, this seemingly arbitrary complexity invites us to look for what may be a more simple reason why the church flourishes in environments of persecution.

To begin with, we should not overstate the growth of the early Church by comparison with other movements.

Hirsch estimates that the church grew from 25,000 in AD 100 to about 20,000,000 in AD 310. This would reflect a 38% growth per decade during the intervening period, which is quite impressive, but not unique in the growth of movements.[15] The truth is that any movement that gains lasting traction has tremendous growth in its infancy, when its message is largely unknown to the surrounding population. This is true whether the movement itself is new or whether it is breaking into a new region in which it is unfamiliar. Many US Christian denominations may be stagnant within the United States but are growing in Latin America and Africa. The same sort of situation may help to account for the rapid growth of the church in China during the mid-20th century.

Nonetheless, it is still undeniable that the church has always seemed to thrive under persecution. The early church father Tertullian famously said that the blood of the martyrs is the seed of the Church. While Hirsch may be correct that some aspects of apostolic genius take over in the absence of institutionalism, there may also be simpler reasons why the church tends to grow under persecution, apart from one fact that shouldn't be ignored: God may supernaturally intervene on behalf of the church

---

[15] It is significantly less, for example, than the 48% growth per decade claimed by the Mormon church between 1840 and 2010. This is taken from the LDS statistics, reflecting 16,865 adherents in 1840 and over 14 million in 2010. These statistics are sometimes said to be inflated. However, the Mormon church could be inflating its recent statistics by almost two-thirds and still match the growth rate of the early Christian church. My point is not to laud the LDS church for its growth rate, but rather to point out the exponential growth that movements demonstrate during their early years, prior to saturation.

when it is under persecution, simply because it's to his glory to display his strength when we are powerless.

Apart from supernatural explanations, one reason why the church grows under persecution may simply be that in situations where persecution is taking place, the entire population is often being stressed, not only the Christians within it. This was certainly the case for the Chinese people suffering under the Cultural Revolution. Similarly, the rise of Christianity took place during a period of significant cultural upheaval in the Roman Empire, as the Roman population lost faith in the traditional gods of ancient Greece and Rome and a number of mystery religions competed for the attention of people looking for alternative spiritual answers. Harsh or uncertain conditions at large tend to make people more thoughtful regarding life and death issues, more open to hope coming from supernatural origins.

There may also be another, less obvious reason why the church tends to grow in situations where it is under persecution: when the church has to operate underground, it cannot dominate its adherents' social lives. Anyone trying to encourage outreach in the United States runs into a perennial problem: the longer someone has been in the faith, the more likely it is that that person's entire circle of friends is composed entirely of fellow believers. The reason is simple: churches encourage it—despite what they may advocate when trying to encourage outreach. A church's activities and ministries will tend to grow to occupy as much time as its adherents will give. People tend to continue supporting organizations to which they are giving substantial amounts of time and energy. In American culture, activity equates to relevance, and every local church fears to be the one at which less is going on than at another. So churches and their activities effectively distance their congregations from the people they are attempting to reach.

When someone comes to faith in Jesus, one of the things that happens almost immediately is that the church pulls that person away from former acquaintances, and when a child grows up in a Christian home, he or she is likely to be as insulated as possible from the corrupting influences of the surrounding secular culture. This is largely accomplished by creating a parallel Christian subculture that separates believers out from unbelievers, from childhood on. Many church denominations have some version of Boy Scouts and Girl Scouts, rather than encouraging their children to participate in the official Scouting organizations, and thus mix with unchurched children in a social environment. Parents send their children to Christian schools and even Christian colleges, not necessarily to provide a better education for their children, but to insulate them from unbelieving peers, teachers, and worldviews. We withdraw into a subculture that reaffirms our beliefs and protects us from outside influences, not recognizing that we are also protecting the unbelieving world from our own influence.

Churches under persecution do not have that luxury. Christians can't simply withdraw into a self-contained subculture; they have to rub shoulders with the rest of the world. Even with the threat of official reprisals, actual friendships between believers and unbelievers may still flourish. The opportunity for believers to share their faith—and perhaps more importantly, for them to gain a receptive hearing by living out godly lives while in relationship with unbelievers—is possibly higher than it is when the church is allowed to dominate its people's lives. The problem is only worse in an era of social networking over the internet, in which people already have every incentive not to know their physical neighbors when there is a worldwide network of like-minded people available to confirm one's own thoughts and interests. At this point, it is not only believers who do the self-ghettoizing. Everyone does.

Churches that are not under persecution need to beware of the temptation to dominate our most committed members. We need seriously to take into account the time and energy we expect from the people who attend, not only to avoid burning people out, but to give them space for individual community involvement. What if, instead of having their own choirs, churches encouraged their people who like to sing to join community choirs, and be an influence on people in that group? What if, instead of having our own sports leagues, we chose to become a part of community leagues? What if churches freed up their members' time and actively encouraged them to join chess clubs, community clean up campaigns, volleyball teams, book clubs, and self-improvement classes? What if we didn't try to duplicate all these things and draw people into our alternative version, and instead participated in the version that already exists?

This might be a means of fulfilling what Hirsch calls the missional-incarnational impulse, but while Hirsch draws attention to communities that have been founded with the purposed vision of living among the poor or those who are otherwise neglected by the traditional church, I would advocate an approach that is more accessible to more people who cannot, for practical reasons, simply pick up and move into a completely different way of life. There is no encouragement in Acts or in the epistles for believers to make significant employment or residence changes in order to reach others—except, of course, for those who became traveling ministers because God had called them to an apostolic or evangelistic ministry. As a matter of fact, Paul gives exactly the opposite advice in 1 Corinthians 7:17, writing, "Each person should live as a believer in whatever situation the Lord has assigned to them, just as God has called them." We may also look at the response John the Baptist gave to tax collectors and soldiers who asked him what life changes they should be making as a result of their repentance. He told them not to change professions, but rather to conduct their professions with honor and integrity (Luke 3:12-14). So rather than making a drastic change in order to live as a missionary in a neglected subculture—which some people, to be sure, will be called and gifted to do, and they should be encouraged and empowered to do it—most believers should take advantage of their own interests and abilities, using them among others in the world, rather than exclusively within the church. That means that the church will have to stop trying to duplicate what the world is already doing and give its people both time and encouragement to participate in their own communities.

The idea is to get out among the world and be a part of it, reflecting Jesus where we are, rather than trying to draw the world into our own tightly-controlled subculture. Could it be messy? Might we actually have to deal with—gasp!—*beer* at the events we take part in? Sure. We can also be the people who don't get drunk at the event. We can be the people who don't badmouth our spouses and who speak positively when others are being negative.

This doesn't mean that we have to be looking for the opportunity to give a full-blown evangelistic message to those with whom we rub shoulders in this way. None of this invalidates what has already been said about giftedness and various zones of influence. But simply being a believer among people who aren't, giving them a taste of a different sort of life, can be a powerful thing.

From my own admittedly limited experience, it appears that most churches that espouse a missional strategy are still trying to coordinate events and outreaches themselves instead of simply encouraging and teaching their members to be involved in the world and be salt and light while they're there. We talk about being the church outside the walls of the building and outside of Sunday services, but it still seems that we don't accept missional outreach as being valid unless it's being structured and coordinated by the organized church, which takes a lot more time, effort, energy, and money than simply being Jesus in the social world that already exists.

What prevents us from doing this is the pesky issue of control. We can't control what we don't originate, plan, schedule, and coordinate. We can't keep tabs on people when they are at some event that members of the church leadership aren't at. We can't evaluate people on the basis of their participation in our events when they're not our events. And we can't insulate and protect people from the influence of the world if we're actively encouraging them to be in it.

But we also can't influence the world if we don't do just that. When the church is under persecution, it loses that control by force. It doesn't have the luxury of creating elaborate evangelism strategies, outreach efforts, attractional events, or other deliberate means of trying to draw in new people. It's focused on survival and on the spiritual growth of the people it already touches. It's also looking toward reaching others, but because the effort has to be underground, most types of overt evangelism are already off the table. But people live their lives, not in the church, but in the world. They are in the world, but not of it, which is exactly the Apostle Paul's prescription.

What About Churches That Don't Do Outreach?

Throughout this book, I've been making the case that outreach and evangelism tend not only to be ineffective, but in the long run prove to be counterproductive, at least in the way that most evangelical churches approach these efforts. This raises a very reasonable question: why, then, don't churches grow when they *don't* actively evangelize or promote outreach programs? Everyone knows that there are plenty of churches—probably the majority—that have little to no serious outreach going on, and they are not obviously outgrowing churches that do. In fact, a cursory glance at churches in general would support the idea that most very small churches don't do much evangelism, if any, while most larger churches have outreach efforts taking place on a regular basis. This, by itself, would seem to invalidate the central idea of this book.

The short answer to this question would be that most churches that have little to no outreach going on are usually afflicted with deeper problems that also stifle growth—in fact, stifle it much more than a misdirected effort toward evangelism would. The problem with the typical outreach mentality is not that it is wrong, but that it is too narrowly focused. It tries to channel every believer into producing conversions, rather than letting every believer participate in the larger process of bringing people from outright hostility toward God to a full, deep, rich, growing, mature relationship with him. What afflicts most churches that aren't centered on evangelism is either a complete lack of direction or an emphasis on things that are foreign to the purpose and role that God gave to the church.

One of the things that can afflict such a church is an unhealthy concentration on tradition. Tradition is a complex thing that most ministers refuse to deal with as complex—it's either embraced as the essence of what the religious life is all about, or it's rejected as nothing but an impediment to change and renewal. Tradition is a little like the bronze snake that Moses made and put up on a pole so that people who had been bitten by venomous snakes could look to it and live (Num. 21:4-9). This was something that God had commanded Moses to do, and it worked, but the bronze snake later had to be destroyed by Hezekiah, because it was being treated like an idol (2 Kings 18:4). Nonetheless, it was important enough in a positive sense that Jesus used it as a symbol of his own crucifixion (John 3:14).

Religious tradition begins as worship. Worship has to take a form in order to exist at all: it necessarily involves some sort of physical action, even though what we're doing—lifting our hands, kneeling, singing, lying prostrate, lighting candles, responsive reading, dancing—is merely an outward expression of the worship we're truly conducting within our spirits. The Bible heartily encourages such expressions of worship. The danger lies in confusing a specific form of worship with worship itself—mistaking the outward expression for the inward reality.

When a person or a church adopts a particular form of worship, that form tends to become traditional—it's the way that person always expresses worship, or the type of worship that is expected in that church. There's nothing inherently wrong with worship expressing itself in a familiar form, because familiarity allows us to stop concentrating on the form and use it to express worship to God. As C. S. Lewis wrote in *Letters to Malcolm,* "As long as you notice, and have to count, the steps, you are not yet dancing but only learning to dance." Once you've learned the dance—or the worship style—it can become a means of expression. But the opposite can happen. The form itself rises to primary importance, and the worship it is supposed to express gets forgotten. Many churches are in this position, paralyzed by an encrustation of forms that have long ago lost all of the live meaning they once had. This can encompass everything from décor to musical style, preaching approach to congregational participation, as well as expected weekly, monthly, and annual events, all of which can suck time, energy, and effort from the real work of the church.

Churches that become overly traditional focus on things that used to have meaning but don't anymore, that used to express true worship but now are merely self-perpetuating rituals. This is true no matter what types of traditions are being discussed—traditions aren't necessarily old! People who attend such churches expect a specific type of service format and calendar of events. Regardless of whether the format and events still convey worship, or any other central aspect of the purpose of the church, they are nonetheless expected, and woe to the person who attempts to introduce change!

It's easy to see why these churches don't attract people. They're not intended to. They're focused on catering to the tastes of the longest-tenured members, and offer nothing life-giving to their own younger generations, let alone to the outside world. They concentrate neither on outreach to the lost nor on the discipleship and development of their own members. They merely provide a very targeted form of religious satisfaction for a specific segment of the population: those who are already there.

Another reason for the lack of growth in non-outreaching churches lies in the power of self-perception. Most evangelical churches, even if they don't actively pursue evangelism and outreach themselves, still believe that their function *ought* to be outreach. Most pastors whose gifts and passions are not evangelistic in nature still subscribe to a view of the Great Commission that obligates them, at least in theory, to intentional outreach. Therein lies the trouble. A church that believes that its essential function is to be a missions outpost to its community, even if it doesn't act on that belief, will have a hard time flourishing because it is based on a misguided self-perception. In these types of churches, there is often the pervasive feeling of failure. Pastors of these churches often carry a double dose of guilt, feeling that they are failing both as individuals and as leaders.

This kind of misperception is double-edged: not only does it create a sense of unfulfilled obligation, but it also prevents those same leaders from wholeheartedly pursuing avenues of ministry for which they are truly gifted and passionate. They may be undercutting their own message with a false note of outreach rhetoric; they may encounter criticism from other ministers who don't recognize the value of the ministry that they are passionate about; they may simply feel that they ought to soft-pedal what they've always been told was an enthusiasm that should be secondary to reaching the lost with the gospel. This is probably a hurdle most difficult for solo pastors, who feel the responsibility to deliver all expected aspects of ministry themselves, but they can also be a problem for staff pastors at larger churches, because positions are usually not divided up according to giftedness and passion, but rather according to demographics: children, youth, couples, singles, young families, seniors, etc. A multistaff church should be an opportunity for each staff pastor to specialize in specific areas of giftedness and passion, but this opportunity is lost when each pastor essentially does the same thing for a different group of people.

A final reason why churches that are not focused on outreach do not grow, related to the first two, is that the majority of churches that are not active outreach communities are also not effective discipling communities either. A church that is actively discipling people and encouraging all types of gifting is not anti-evangelism: it should have some members that are gifted and motivated toward outreach, and those members should be encouraged. This lack of discipleship is most often related to the focus on tradition discussed earlier, but it can also be related to leadership that is focused neither on evangelism nor discipleship but rather has some other center of attention. Some pastors have a passion for service to the needy; others demonstrate a prophetic bent, challenging ungodly attitudes and practices in society or the church; still others love to counsel and minister healing to individuals, couples, and relationships. All of these are valid gifts and deeply needed in the body of Christ. Not all of them lend themselves to positions of leadership, unless the person gifted in a particular way also has the capacity not only to do the ministry but also to assist others to do it, and work with others to develop people with different gifts. In the typical paradigm of evangelicalism, serious devotion to God tends to lead to some form of pastoral ministry, which is not always a good fit. Ephesians identifies pastors as one among several types of leadership; Romans names leadership itself as one among many gifts. Not everyone called to ministry is called to pastoral ministry.

Without intending to, ministers who have a focus on something other than evangelism or discipleship often treat ministry as a form of self-expression. The mercy pastor—especially one in full-time ministry—may take the week in between Sunday services as his opportunity to serve people who are in need, neglecting aspects of ministry needed to benefit the whole body. Prophetic pastors may use the sermon to express outrage at particular forms of ungodliness, and tend to attract people who are similarly outraged, and who can avoid dealing with their own problems by focusing on others' sins. Prophetic pastors may also sometimes attract the sort of person that has a perverse enjoyment in being made to feel guilty, but is not thereby delivered and empowered to live out the gospel in a better way. Counselor pastors may be particularly effective in interpersonal communication but less effective in pulpit ministry or administration. Even pastors who focus on discipleship may impede the evangelism that should be inherent within it if they have a deficient view of what discipleship is, and don't give rein for those who do have gifts in evangelism and outreach to express that passion.

Not giving rein to those who are passionate about evangelism is, actually, more common than one might think. Despite giving lip service to reaching the lost, some pastors—particularly solo pastors—are already overwhelmed with burdens from their existing congregations, either in terms of individual needs or in terms of traditional expectations within that local church. Although it would be seldom ever stated in so many words, the actual prospect of more people coming in with more needs and expectations may be felt by some pastors to be more of a burden than an opportunity, so growth is subtly squelched even as it is espoused publicly as a goal. Such a pastor may also feel obligated to lead any evangelistic effort taking place, and not have the energy to do so, or may resist the lack of control involved with handing the reins of such an undertaking over to someone more gifted to do it. It is simply unthinkable, in many churches, for any significant effort to take place without the pastor (or one of the staff pastors) leading it.

It is important, as we discuss reasons for churches not growing, that we don't lapse back into a view that regards numerical growth as the sole or even the primary means of measuring ministry success. Some of types of ministry may create growth, even if it is unhealthy, in an individual local church. And there's no guarantee of growth for churches doing ministry the right way—even if a right way could be perfectly determined. Jesus' ministry widely fluctuated in the numbers of people it attracted (John 6). The real test of whether a church is operating in a way that is biblical and God-honoring is not numerical growth, but rather the degree to which people's lives are being transformed into the image of Christ in their actions, attitudes, and worldview. Are they understanding their faith in ways consistent with the doctrinal sections of the epistles? Are they exhibiting character consistent with the paranetic sections of the epistles? Are they working together in harmony, doing different things but with one unified purpose, as the body is supposed to function?

Ultimately, ministry is about faithfulness, not success, an extremely difficult thing to learn in an American culture driven by achievement. No matter what measure we try to use, a success mentality is ultimately based on self. If our question is, "What must I do for my church to be successful?" we're very close to the rich young ruler's question, "What must I do to inherit eternal life?" (Mark 10:17). The focus is on us and our performance, our technique, our strategy, our ability. We need to wrench that focus off of ourselves and onto God's faithfulness to us through Jesus, and our joyful surrender to his will and service to his kingdom.

Reimagining Outreach

The evangelical church is theoretically committed to outreach and evangelism, whether or not it actually does anything about it. Local churches tend to view themselves as missions outposts, regardless of whether they actually do any actual evangelistic or missional work in their communities. More to the point, many churches that sincerely attempt to do something about their commitment to outreach—churches that teach evangelism strategies or conduct evangelistic events, churches that run soup kitchens and homeless shelters, churches that have special concerts, sporting events, plays, and services to draw in unchurched people, churches that do special service projects and outreach events—many, in fact the vast majority, don't see lasting growth as a result of doing these things. A huge amount of time, effort, and energy is being expended in order to reach out, centered on bringing more people into the body of Christ—but that result is not taking place.

Something is wrong.

Individual churches sometimes think that what is wrong is other churches. Their church is the only one doing what's right. Those other churches, those other so-called Christians, have left such a bad impression that one church's efforts have to overcome huge obstacles in order to make any headway at all. People have been so burned by the unloving, legalistic, apathetic, judgmental, uncaring, boring, inward-directed, tradition-bound churches in the surrounding area, that they've made outreach almost impossible. Of course, that church may be saying something similar about yours.

Eventually, church leaders tend to turn on their own members. Nobody is committed enough. People don't have a heart for the lost. They aren't willing to pay the price. They aren't willing to come out of their comfort zones. Leaders try seeker-sensitive service formats and sermon topics that will minister to the felt needs of those in their surrounding area. They try sermon series intended to teach their people methods of outreach. They appeal to their congregations' sense of guilt. Finally, they harangue and lash out in frustration, because they had set out with noble ambitions to change the world, and it's not happening.

Meanwhile, congregations become progressively de-moralized. They love Jesus, they want to serve him, they want to see more people follow him, they especially want to see their loved ones find him, but most of them feel like a fish out of water actually doing it. Their efforts don't bear fruit. They see some people being obnoxious in their efforts to witness, and they don't want to be like that. They feel guilty, but various techniques and strategies that (they are told) work well for other people seem not to work for them. There must be something wrong with them, they inwardly conclude. So they just shut down.

Sometimes pastors change churches, thinking that the particular congregation they're leading is simply hard-hearted, unwilling to change and reach out. They go to another congregation with new energy and vitality and a new group of people who seem much more receptive. But over time, the old pattern reasserts itself. Perhaps growth was happening for a while, but then stalls. Maybe key families move away. The church seems in decline again. The pastor focuses on outreach, which doesn't get off the ground. The people just don't seem to get the importance of it. Thoughts of moving on, or quitting, once more trouble the minds of pastors caught in this loop.

Sometimes lay people change churches. They're tired of being beaten over the head. They're looking for a place of worship with some vitality and life, affirmation rather than condemnation. They're looking for something to hope for, something worth believing in, and for a while they think they've found it. Often this will be a newly founded church, or a church with a new pastor. But eventually they find themselves in the same situation, hearing the same messages. The only thing that really matters is saving souls. The only reason you're here on this earth is to lead people to Christ. The old familiar guilt comes back. They begin to think of moving on again. But after a few cycles, there's not that much hope that things will be different anywhere. So they stay, but withdraw, and become a part of the apparently apathetic church culture that their pastors are railing against.

These pastors, looking for ways to motivate their congregations toward outreach and evangelism, wondering if they could be more effective in another setting, are not necessarily bad people or even bad leaders. The people in their congregations, burned out by one program after another, feeling ineffective, unfulfilled, and guilty— they're not necessarily bad people, either. They're just all caught in a bad paradigm of ministry.

They are, or used to be, actually passionate about some things. They may be people who love to serve, or love to teach, or love to build things for people, or create works of art, or write. Maybe they play a musical instrument— and they may or may not be inclined to do worship music. Maybe they like to help out with projects behind the scenes, or maybe they naturally gravitate toward leadership roles. Maybe they enjoy nurturing children. Many church leaders will assert that *of course* we need people with all these different talents. We have a place for everyone! We're always in need of people who will use their talents and gifts for Jesus!

But that's not the message that people hear. What they hear is, "We welcome and encourage you to use your gifts in the church—*and* you need to evangelize. It's great that you minister to kids—but what are you doing about the lost? You volunteer at a soup kitchen? That's great! Why don't you think about leaving that and starting a new ministry to the homeless under the headship of our church? That's a nice short story you've written—maybe you want to beef up the salvation message a bit?"

You're good. Just not good enough.

Everything is focused on the bottom line of reaching people. It's not good enough to use your talents and gifts as a blessing to others: they either have to be in some way directly connected with bringing unbelievers to Christ, or else they're a harmless side interest—harmless as long as you make sure you're not neglecting the Great Commission. It's not good enough to practice a skill or a hobby out in the marketplace with the world; it has to be done under the auspices and direction of the organizational church. It's not good enough to write or paint or compose something that expresses true feelings and thoughts from a Christian perspective—there has to be a message, some didactic purpose that could bring people to Christ, or help equip believers to do so.

In short, American evangelical Christians are not encouraged *at all* to become mature, well-rounded, fully formed, unique individuals, because all that is just a distraction from the overriding mission of reaching people for Christ. But precisely because they are not encouraged to grow in who they are, because their passions and talents are not esteemed, because they have a different mandate laid on them—one that is arguably not what Jesus had in mind or what the Bible directs them to do as individuals—their very passion for reaching the lost is weakened, not strengthened. The imperative to outreach is not merely ineffective; it's actually counterproductive.

Maybe it's not the people in this scenario that are the problem. Maybe it's the model.

Maybe we could envision a different model, one in which an important goal of the whole *is* to make disciples of all nations, but in which making disciples is thought of as a much larger transformation of people, and in which each individual plays a smaller and a different part. Maybe people's gifts and talents should be thought worthy of pursuit for their own sake, trusting that if God made them with those passions, and if they love him, they will channel those talents into avenues that are God-honoring and have a positive effect on those who are touched by them. Maybe doing good in the community will be thought of as a godly thing, even if it comes with no evangelistic hook. Maybe discipling someone who is already a believer will be thought of as being as important in the process as guiding someone through a sinner's prayer. Maybe most outreach from the church into the world will not be organized and controlled by the church leadership at all, but will be a result of believers involving themselves in non-religious organizations and events, simply being salt and light in those places.

Maybe the organizational church will understand that individuals' time is not unlimited, that space needs to be given in order to allow people to be able to devote energy outside the church, and that this outside interaction should be recognized as doing the work of the Kingdom, not as a distraction from doing the work of the church. Maybe, as every believer is encouraged to become mature and uniquely developed, they will feel empowered and engaged in whatever portion of the Great Commission God has designed them to fulfill. It's okay for Paul to plant and Apollos to water. We can trust God to give the increase.

What this will take, quite frankly, is a reimagining of the church's goals, methods, and structure. The goal will need to be that of personal transformation of every individual, not only in terms that appear "spiritual," but also aesthetic and practical. We're looking for well-rounded, healthy, functional, whole persons, not simply units of the Borg that are able to assimilate others. The goal will be measured not merely by how many people are transformed, but also (and even more importantly) *how much* they are transformed. And evaluating that is going to be complex, because people are different. One person's maturity isn't going to look like another person's maturity. But when we recognize maturity, we will need to celebrate people exhibiting *their gifts* in that context, not determining how much they deviate from an expected standard.

The church's methods will also need to be examined. The missional movement has already critiqued the attractional nature of the traditional church. Our goal should be to move out into the world and be Jesus there, not try to suck people into our world. Many churches seem to embrace the rhetoric but not the reality of this approach. We want to have specified missional outreaches in order ultimately to attract people, even if we may understand this to be a long-term process. Although our intentions might be missional, the way we go about those intentions reveals our discomfort with that approach. We want specified events that we have designed and planned, in which we coordinate people as we see fit, in order to accomplish a goal that we've decided on. We're not really going out into the world at all. We're sending a squadron into enemy territory, but the squadron still remains a part of the organized church. It's a bubble that temporarily goes out, tries to accomplish something, and comes back again. This is why, when the leadership of a church talks about its people's commitment to outreach, it focuses on its people's participation in the outreach events coordinated by the church. What you do on your own time doesn't count.

And this is where the organization of the church comes into play. If we're really encouraging our congregations to be salt and light in the world, then we need to give them the freedom to be in the world, although not of it. We, as the church, need to participate in the world's structures, not impose our own. One would think that this would appeal to churches strapped for resources. Someone else does the planning, funding, and organization— we just jump on board and represent Christ. But in fact, this idea doesn't even occur to most church leaders, because it involves giving up control. It runs the very real risk that "our" people will not only be in the world, but will choose to become of it as well. We may lose people. Guess what? We're losing people already.

So what would a truly discipling church of the type I'm discussing look like? I have no specific prescription, just some general ideas.

The church would, first of all, be focused on the broad scope of the Great Commission, from pre-evangelism through full maturity, rather than being focused narrowly on conversion. Success would be measured by the extent to which lives were changed, not merely the number of adherents that were attracted—although success itself would be less focused on than faithfulness. Maturity would be recognized by the degree to which people develop into unique members with unique gifts that function for the good of the body—it would not be focused on a single standard based on the leaders' own gifts, passions, and ambitions.

So if we're going to orient a church around its members' gifts, the types of programs, events, and outreaches that are possible will be dictated neither by traditional expectations of what a church should offer, nor by a leadership brainstorming session on what a new model of church should look like. Instead, it would be determined by the talents and passions of the people who are there. In the early stages, this might look like a bizarre hodgepodge. There might be a men's group but not a women's group. There might be teachers for infants and teens but not for children in between. There might not be any of these traditional types of ministries, but something entirely different, unique to your fellowship. Here's the point: ministries are created by responding to people's passions and empowering them to carry those passions out, rather than being created out of perceived need.

The typical thing that happens in churches is that ministries are created as a response to perceived needs, and then the leadership prays for the necessary positions to be filled with passionate people. We have a children's church because every church is supposed to have a children's church; we have a men's group because the pastor wants to have a men's group; and we do these things whether or not there are gifted people to lead them. And churches are always looking for people to fill positions because the ministry was created before a gifted person was found to lead it, or continued on after a gifted leader left. People who want to be supportive find themselves in ministries they're neither passionate about nor talented in, which is a recipe for frustration and burnout.

On the other hand, if we frankly choose from the outset that the ministries we have will be the ones that people are already passionate about, then there will always be just the right person for whatever ministry exists, because the ministry exists in response to that person's passion and ability to do it. Moreover, getting everyone involved in ministry would no longer be a problem, because people are not being asked to do anything that they are not already passionate about doing. This is not simply a matter of enabling people's desire for self-expression. It is recognizing that God has placed those gifts and those passions in each person's life in order to benefit the church in a way that only that person can.

This model might seem ridiculously naïve in churches that are continually trying to get people to fill positions. "You'll never find enough people who are passionate about all the things that need to be done." But what's being suggested requires far less superstructure than a typical church, because we would not be concerning ourselves with a ton of extraneous things that need to be done, but rather simply allowing people who are already motivated to do what they want to do.

In terms of church gatherings themselves, I'd suggest a single weekly meeting—just as the early Christians followed the example of the synagogue service. The main purpose of this meeting is not outreach, which eliminates the seeker sensitive model, because an evangelistically-focused weekly service does little to further the Great Commission among most of the people who attend. Focus a service on the development of the disciples who are there, and seekers will rise to the challenge, seeing that there's something beyond conversion to look forward to. Focus a service on the felt needs of the seekers who are there, and you run into the TV news problem of continually feeding the "what's in it for me" mentality. There can always be an invitation at the end of a service, or an offer to meet with pastors (or better yet gifted and empowered evangelists). If we understand conversion to be a process and not an emotional decision, we won't be concerned with letting an opportunity slip by. The real purpose of the weekly service is to instruct, build up, inspire, and enable people who are already believers to go out, exercise their gifts, and live their lives in a Christ-honoring way in the world around them.

Apart from the weekly service, I'd only recommend a small group meeting for discipleship, once every week or two. As described in the chapter on discipleship, these meetings can be of a great many varieties. Groups for new believers will be very similar, getting people a basic understanding of the Bible and the basics of the Christian life. As people grow into maturity, groups will become more diverse, reflecting the gifts and talents that are developing in each person. Groups are intended not merely as conveyors of information, but more importantly, developers of relationships in which people can find encouragement, counsel, support, and wisdom. The goal is not for the leader to reproduce people just like himself, but to facilitate the development of each person into his or her own greatest potential. Along with meeting in groups, one-on-one friendships and mentorships should develop, because that is where deep intimate discipleship can take place.

The real goal here, though, is not to build a mass of people who attend services and small groups. The goal is to encourage them to use whatever gifts or talents they have in the surrounding community. This is not merely toleration; it's active encouragement for everyone to involve themselves in classes, clubs, teams, organizations, and activities, for the purpose of enjoying the activity itself (this is important) as well as being a Christian influence in the world.

This won't apply to everyone equally. As we saw with the continuum model, there are some people whose primary mission will be to other believers—that's what they've been gifted for. But most people will have some sort of interest through which they could make natural contacts with those who aren't disciples yet. The point is for these contacts to be natural—each person is genuinely pursuing an interest that will bring them into contact with other people with similar interests. From that point, the goal isn't to look for opportunities to wedge Jesus into the conversation; the goal is simply to live out one's life as a believer around nonbelievers. At some point, someone who is open to the gospel will open up the opportunity themselves. Then, the believer is in the position of responding, not pushing their beliefs on others. Or perhaps a person who has been opened up to the gospel through social interaction with believers will encounter through God's providence a person with more evangelistic gifts and be prepared to listen and respond.

This is different from traditional outreach because it's not designed and coordinated by the church. It's important that the church *not* duplicate the clubs, teams, and organizations that the world offers, because while it's easy for believers to join organizations in the world, it's extremely difficult to get anyone other than believers to join the church's equivalent. As stated earlier, the organizational church loses control but gains access to many people who wouldn't darken the door of a church; it risks people being affected and perhaps being drawn away, but that risk is inherent in Paul's counsel that we be in, although not of, the world.

Many churches would protest that *of course* they want their people to involve themselves in the world—they're always challenging people to form friendships with nonbelievers. But that's impossible when the church has multiple services, fellowship groups, discipleship classes, committee meetings, "outreach" events, service projects, and other various opportunities for its most committed members to have their time sucked away from any meaningful interaction with the outside world.

When we involve ourselves in the world's organizations, we not only create relationships which may lead to sharing the gospel with others—or at least living out godly character among others in our community—but we also get the opportunity to develop whatever talent or skill that interested us in that organization in the first place. What does this have to do with the Great Commission or the mission of the church? Everything, if we recognize that God wants us to become whole, well-rounded people and not just convert-making machines. Whatever makes us more ourselves and develops our gifts and talents helps us become more specialized instruments that God can use in whatever way he sees fit.

It's time we look toward being healthy, whole, and mature, and leave the increase up to God. It's time that pastors focus on feeding, encouraging, and nurturing the people God has given them, instead of focusing on the people they haven't been given yet. It's time we allowed people to become the people God made them to be, with all their differences and uniqueness. It's time we focused on feeding the sheep, and let God worry about them multiplying.

Because doing what God told us to do is our job. Controlling the outcome is his.

About the Author

Keith Edwin Schooley grew up in the Detroit area. He attended Wayne State University where he began as a physics major and ended with an honors English degree. He worked as an editor for Gale Research, Inc. on their *Twentieth-Century Literary Criticism* series before leaving to earn a Master's degree in New Testament Studies from Gordon-Conwell Theological Seminary in South Hamilton, Massachusetts. He and his wife Cecile together have six children.

Keith has pastored a church in Brimley, a small town in Michigan's upper peninsula; taught literature and biblical studies at William Tyndale College and at the Assemblies of God Central Bible College; counseled and taught at the Teen Challenge Training Center in Rehrersburg, Pennsylvania; and presently lives with his family in the Detroit area.

Points of Contact

schooleyfiles.com
facebook.com/KeithEdwinSchooley
twitter.com/keschooley
linkedin.com/in/keithschooley

Made in the USA
Charleston, SC
17 November 2013